THE IRVINEBANK MASSACRE

PAUL DILLON

Connor Court Publishing

Published in 2021 by Connor Court Publishing Pty Ltd

Copyright © Paul Dillon 2021

All rights reserved. No part of this book may be reproduced or transmitted in any form or by any means, electronic or mechanical, including photocopying, recording or by any information storage and retrieval system, without prior permission in writing from the publisher.

Connor Court Publishing Pty Ltd
PO Box 7257
Redland Bay QLD 4165
sales@connorcourt.com
www.connorcourtpublishing.com.au

Phone 0497-900-685

Printed in Australia

ISBN 9781922449498

Front Cover image: Samuel Thomas Gill. Native Police, or Black Trackers on a trail, [1842-1872], courtesy of Dixson Library, State Library of New South Wales.

Tags: Queensland Colonial history, 19th century Queensland criminal justice system, social and political history of 19th century Queensland, Native Police, Queensland Police, Aborigines and 19th century white settler/Aborigine conflict.

About the Author

Paul Dillon is a Sunshine Coast based author of *Frederick Walker Commandant of the Native Police*, Connor Court Publishing, Brisbane 2018; *The Murder of John Francis Dowling and the Massacre of 300 Aborigines*, Connor Court Publishing, Brisbane 2019; Inside the *Killing Fields Hornet Bank, Cullin-la-Ringo & The Maria Wreck*, Connor Court Publishing, Brisbane 2020; Queensland Native Police, The First Twenty Years, 2020 and Red Centre, Dead Centre *The True Story of Peter Falconer*, Austin Macauley Publisher, London 2019. He holds a Bachelor of Arts degree from the Australian National University. Paul joined the Commonwealth Public Service in 1965. On 23 May 1986, he was called to the Bar of New South Wales and practised as a barrister in the Criminal Division of the superior courts of Queensland as counsel for the defence.

Contents

Introduction		7
1	Irvinebank	13
2	Police Presence	35
3	Inquest	41
4	Committal Proceedings	47
5	Public Comment	71
6	Academic Treatment	95
7	Conclusion	109
Appendix A		124
Bibliography and Abbreviations		135

Introduction

This monograph is about the murder of four Aborigines on top of a mountain outside the township of Irvinebank in far north Queensland. The murders occurred on Saturday evening, 18 October 1884 at the campsite of the Aborigines. The victims were King Billy, Kitty, one other female and a piccaninny, sex unknown. The murders caused an outrage amongst the white community of the Herberton district and were sensationalised in the Brisbane press. An inquest was held and suspicion fell upon the native troopers of the Nigger Creek Native Police (NP) detachment. A police investigation was conducted which led to the arrest of seven native troopers. They were committed to stand trial for the murders but the charge of murder against the troopers was dropped and they were allowed to go free. The white officer in command of the troopers, Sub-Inspector William Nichols was also charged as an accessory before the fact to the murders by his troopers. The court found he had no case to answer.

The question is how might this incident, if it were of historical significance or interest, be written up in the annals of Australia's colonial history? First of all, the incident involved Aborigines killing Aborigines; secondly, none of the Aborigines involved could speak English and thirdly, they all appeared to have been full-blood, initiated, tribal blacks. The only element connecting the incident to colonial white Australia was the fact that the native troopers were in the service of the colony of Queensland. The other significant dimension to the incident is that there are no aboriginal sources, either in language or otherwise, of the event. The sources for the event are all written in English and are all predicated on a Eurocentric perspective.

The accused native troopers were members of the Queensland Native Police who were part of the Queensland Police Force. They operated under a set of regulations known as the Native Police Regulations as published in Queensland Government Gazette of 10 March 1866.[1] The Native Police were seen as a preventive force that protected settlers, pastoralists and miners from the depredations of myall blacks in the outside or unsettled districts of the colony. Their operational role was defined in the regulations as follows:

> 17. The object in sending out patrol parties is principally that the hostile blacks, from the frequent visits of the police, may be deterred from murder and felony – this is the meaning of a preventive force.

---

[1] Vol. VII. 10 March 1866. [No. 28.] pp 258-261.

INTRODUCTION

The troop left Nigger Creek under the command of Sub-Inspector William Nichols who was accompanied by Cadet Officer Walter Garraway. The troop entered Irvinebank on 17 October 1884 and pitched their tents within the town and camped the night there. On the morning of 18 October 1884, they were paraded by Nichols and corporal Sambo, a native trooper, was instructed to take the other six troopers and "Catch Tommy and mind you don't use your rifles." The two-white officers of police remained in camp. The troopers left on horseback in uniform armed with Snider rifles and a cartridge belt each.

That evening they returned to camp and Nichols addressed Sambo as follows, "You bring in Tommy, Sambo?"

He replied, "No catch em marme, think em gone away." The troop returned to Nigger Creek NP camp on 19 October 1884.

What is history: The attempt to tell the facts of the incident honestly and accurately or the conclusions drawn from the facts?

The only acknowledged study of this incident by an academic, concluded from the facts of the incident that "The Native Mounted Police represented virtually the sum total of Colonial Queensland's policy towards its indigenous people for half a century and it was unarguably a policy primarily based on collective punishment without trial; one that was not only illegal, but morally bankrupt."[2]

---

[2] *Failure of Justice: the story of the Irvinebank Massacre* / written by Geof Genever; additional information written by Duncan Ray, Tony Derksen [and] Henry Tranter, Malanda, Qld.: Eacham Historical Society, Reprint Second Edition, May 2010 p 16.

The editor of the *Herberton Advertiser* concluded as follows:

> That the Native Trooper Corps have a deterrent effect has been proved in this district, but that its dismemberment without substitutes on a reformed system, will bring sorrow and grief to the community we regret to have to predict. Yet that the officer in charge, under the existing system, should be held amenable for the atrocities perpetrated in his absence by semi-civilised savages sent in pursuit to apprehend a deserter of the same colour but of a different tribe and consequently looked upon as a natural enemy, appears anomalous. The evidence adduced shows that the Blacks were instructed to bring in a deserter named "Tommy." Now, who can tell who were "Tommy's" friends and what cropped up to cause the unfortunate slaughter of the innocent blacks at Irvinebank. The latter may or may not have interfered between Tommy and the Troopers, or for causes undivulged the natural animosity between tribes may have incited those possessing firearms to shoot down those who had none, and what appears to the British mind an act of cowardice may have a contrary interpretation by aboriginal custom.[3]

The academic obviously belonged to the Black Armband school of thought for he could only construe the incident as a brutal example of failed government policy and even went to the lengths of calling the incident a massacre.

Australian colonial history since the time of Whitlam has been promulgated by a bunch of cultural misfits akin to a Red Guard movement but known in Australia as the Black Armband Brigade. As a result, Australian history has gone through a cultural revolution of as yet, an uncertain degree of destructive force. Whether the pen-

---
3   28 January 1885, Vol. V. No. 8, see pages 85 & 87 below.

dulum will swing back, who knows? The Black Armband Brigade is concerned with seizing control of Australian history and destroying Australia's white colonial past, including its pioneering myths, folklore and artefacts and the monuments of notable white Australian figures. There was a time when Australia was in harmony, with all the old familiar countervailing forces such as Protestants against Catholics and the Movement (Groupers and DLP) against the communist inspired ALP, finely balanced. The fundamentals of society such as race, religion, gender and role models were settled. It was just a matter of picking up the cards you were dealt and making a go of it.

1

Irvinebank

Irvinebank is a small historic village located in far north Queensland which forms part of the scenic circuit for touring visitors and wandering grey nomads. It is 80 km south-west of Cairns. Established in 1882; it boasts many century old buildings such as the home of John Moffat, Loudoun House, a courthouse and cellblock, the 1901 School of Arts Hall, Tramway Station, the Queensland National Bank Building, Mango Cottage and the 1907 Post Office. In 1880 the Great Northern tin discovery was made at Herberton, 25 km east of Irvinebank. Two years later three prospectors, James Gibb, Andrew Thompson and James McDonald, found promising tin lodes in the catchment of the Gibbs and McDonald Creeks. The Glen Smelting Company in Herberton, managed by John Moffat, acquired several of the tin shows in Gibbs Creek in 1883. In 1883-84 Glen Smelting opened a battery and smelters at Gibbs Creek, renaming it Irvinebank. John Moffat was born in a small village on the Irvine River in Ayrshire, Scotland.

The centres of the Wild River (Herberton) district as at 22 May 1884 were as follows: Herberton, Watsonville, Coolgarra, Irvinebank, Scrubby Creek, Newellton (Silver Valley), Nigger Creek, Eureka Creek, California Creek, the Tate River, Halpin's Creek, Gregory's Gully, Mount Garnet, and Silverfield, the total population being computed at 3500.[4] The total area of land opened for selection in October 1882, was 123,450 acres, and the total selected was 27,500 acres, consisting of 73 homesteads and 41 conditional purchases.

Herberton, the principal town of the district, contained a court house, police quarters, post and telegraph offices, hospital, State school, powder magazine, Roman Catholic and Primitive Methodist chapels, two crushing machines and smelting works. The site of the town was on both sides of the Wild River branching from the original prospecting claim.

Nigger Creek, two and half miles from Herberton, was composed of mineral and agricultural lands; the Monarch Co., the Bradlaugh, and other claims forming the mineral portion. There was a provisional school. The agricultural portion was on the south side of Nigger Creek. E. P. Williams and Co. had an extensive sawing plant at Flaggy Creek. The native police camp and W.R.J.C. race course was in the vicinity of this locality.[5]

---

4   Excluding myall and town Aborigines; their numbers are unknown.
5   *Cairns Post* 22 May 1884 p 3. W.R.J.C. stands for Wild River Jockey Club.

Outrages committed by the Blacks of the Wild River District

A local paper reported as follows:

> On or about 20 May 1881, close to the Great Western, one of the diggers suddenly heard from the bank of the creek immediately over him, a blackfellow singing out, 'Is that you, Jim?' The digger replied, 'Yes,' and looking up, saw a blackfellow, whom he recognised as an old trooper who had run away from the Normanby Camp on the Palmer. The nigger then shouted, 'I mean to do for you,' and immediately threw a spear which struck Jim over the hip. Before the digger could lift his pick to defend himself another spear was thrown which entered his back, cutting across his backbone and tearing the flesh on his ribs. After passing through the flesh the spear entered the fleshy part of his arm, making its way right through. The man, frightened, and in a measure pinioned, made after the black, who made off when he saw the digger 'go for him.' On reaching the camp at the Great Western the spears were drawn out—fortunately only one of them was jagged—the one that passed through his arm. We are informed that the poor fellow is getting on well under the treatment of Mr Nott, of Herberton. The blackfellow who committed the above outrage was dressed in monkey jacket and tweed trousers. He is 'civilised' and speaks good English. Reports have also reached town that another digger had fallen a victim to the blacks a few days previously between the Walsh and Tate rivers. No doubt the old trooper also committed this outrage.[6]

Then on 18 November 1881, two miners, whilst at work at the Western River were speared by two blacks. The wounds were in both cases serious and it was feared that one would prove fatal.[7] The *Telegraph* provided the following harrowing details of the incident:

---

6   *Darling Downs Gazette* 1 June 1881 p 2.
7   *Brisbane Courier* 25 November 1881 p 2.

It was alike, sorrowful and pleasing, to witness the procession on 20 November descending the West Herberton hill, when Mr. Sculler, one of the miners recently speared, was being carried into town in a bush-made but convenient ambulance. The heat was excessive, about 125 in the sun. The stretcher was carried by four stalwart miners, with relays walking at either side, and accompanied by Mr. Long, the chemist. Sculler managed to hold an umbrella to shelter from the broiling sun, but he looked weak and jaded. The miners, upon their arrival at their destination, handled the poor fellow with the gentleness of women; and while the sufferings of the man gave rise to sympathy, a feeling of gladness and pride pervaded the community when they noticed the care with which the strong and healthy miners carried him. On the following day the second man speared, Simpson, was also brought in. The spear completely traversed Sculler's body, and the barb about two inches had to be cut off before it could be withdrawn. The skill and continual attention of Long prolonged his life, but he was in a precarious state. Simpson was not so bad, as the spear did not penetrate through his body; and he was suffering more from the injury done him in the groin with stones, than that caused by the spear. Showing how determined the blacks were to kill their victims, after making sure that Sculler was despatched, they discovered that Simpson was not dead, they then pelted him with chunks of rock, hence the injury causing him the most trouble.[8]

Sub-Inspector Ernest Carr arrived in Herberton with nine troopers on 4 December 1881 from the Barron River, 40 to 45 miles distant, and immediately proceeded to the Western, where the above-mentioned outrages were committed. But some ten days had elapsed since the deed was perpetrated, and there was little or no chance of his getting the right men, although, he might fall in with the blacks who robbed Sculler's effects.

---

8   *Telegraph* 9 December 1881 p 3.

It was further hoped that Mr. Carr might also find the horse stealers who roasted one horse and took away five others; and that he might also find Harry Martin, a missing man.⁹

A Missing Man. A stranger occupying a tent on the Herberton fall, close to Ruined Camp, Western was reported missing since Saturday, 19 November 1881, by a neighbour, a dairyman. The man had recently arrived with his two horses. The latter, including his saddle, bedding, and swag were still at the spot.¹⁰

The whole community was horrified when another atrocious murder was committed by the blacks within four miles of Herberton. The unfortunate victim, Mr. John W. Skene was out looking for his horses on or about 31 March 1882. From the few words the murdered man spoke while dying, the blacks came upon him right on the main road, and ascertaining he had no firearms attacked him. The poor fellow tried to defend himself with his bridle. One spear was driven right through his chest, entering under the arm on the one side and the point just protruding under the other arm. In trying to run away from the blacks, this spear was caught between the trees, and broke off close to the flesh. Another spear was through the shoulder; about 2 inches below the collar-bone, and so firmly embedded that Mr. Long, who attended the dying man, had the greatest difficulty extracting it, and a third into his loins. How the poor fellow escaped the blacks seems astonishing, with four spears in different parts of his body, two in vital parts. Yet he did so, and managed to reach Moss's Horse and Jockey Hotel, about a mile from where he had been attacked, and two miles

---

9   *Telegraph* 9 December 1881 p 3.
10 *Capricornian* 3 December 1881 p 15.

and a-half from Herberton. On arrival, his first request was for a drink of tea; his next that his sister might be sent for, who was in town, and to whom he was very much attached. His brother, Mr. Peter Skene, arrived with her in time to see him die, but not to receive his last words. The poor fellow was too far gone, and could not articulate, though he tried several times to speak to them. He died within an hour or two after the attack upon him. The deceased was a man well known and liked on the field. A large assembly gathered to pay their last respects to the memory of the deceased, and the funeral ceremony of his faith was read over his remains by Mr. John Collins. Sub-Inspector Douglas and his troopers left town the morning after the murder, but returned on 22 April unsuccessful. This was the fifth man speared by the blacks within a mile or two of town.[11]

Then on 20 April it was reported that a reprisal party had been organised on account of the murder of Mr. Skene and general aboriginal aggression. The party dispersed a large camp of twenty-seven blacks and brought in six gins. The native police were wholly ineffective.[12] However, a telegram received by the Commissioner of Police on 25 April stated that there was no truth in the report recently published that six gins were brought into Herberton by a private reprisal party, and further denied that any reprisal party ever went out or was organised.[13]

The carnage at the hands of the blacks continued unabated when it was reported on June 17, 1882, that the blacks of the Herberton scrubs, had been very troublesome at Rifle Creek, about nineteen miles distant. A Mr

---

11   *Queenslander* 22 April 1882 p 486 & *Maryborough Chronicle, Wide Bay and Burnett Advertiser* 29 April 1882 p 4.
12   *Morning Bulletin* 21 April 1882 p 2.
13   *Western Star and Roma Advertiser* 26 April 1882 p 2.

Groves had been a heavy loser—at least forty head of cattle per year. This recent attack had resulted in that gentleman having had eight head killed, besides numbers of others wounded and rushing about in every direction with spears in them.[14]

In an evil hour the Minister for Works promised a road survey from Herberton to Mourilyan. Sub-Inspector Douglas performed the duty and under date, Mourilyan, May 28, 1882 wired to his chief as follows: Fearful trip; no chance of food. Twenty days without rations, living on roots principally. Nineteen days rain without intermission. Brought party through safe; but very weak and suffering from sores. Track marked and cut.[15]

The *Herberton Advertiser* of September 1882 reported that the blacks had been busy spearing horses in the neighbourhood of Beckley's Camp. A miner named Henry Rowe, engaged in searching for his mate's horses, tracked them high into the ranges, where he discovered that two had been killed by the blacks, who cut up and carried away almost every portion of one, and all of the other with the exception of the head and feet. A third, belonging to the same party, came galloping into the camp with a spear through its neck. Thereupon there was a "roll up," and Mr. Beckley, with eight other miners and a blackboy, started to the scene of the butchery to "investigate" the business. The "boy" tracked the depredators to their first and second camps, in each of which they had roasted and feasted upon part of their spoil; but the aboriginal tracker beginning to fancy he was on the scent of some of his own tribe, abandoned the cause of the white Nemesis,

---

14   *Brisbane Courier* 23 June 1882 p 3.
15   *Western Champion* 23 June 1882 p 3

and took to the bush himself. The party, however, continued to follow the trail for fully twenty-six miles, when, having exhausted their rations and lost their sable "guide, counsellor, and friend," they were fain to beat a retreat and make for their camp again.[16]

Two more attempts to murder white men were made by the blacks at no great distance from Herberton and in each case the person attacked was badly speared, narrowly escaping with their life. On 24 September 1882, Mr. William Popple, when returning from the Upper Mulgrave and within two miles of W. Peterson's camp suddenly received a spear from behind, which entered his thigh, rendering him incapable of moving from the spot. Nine spears were thrown at him; one took effect in the thigh. Fortunately, the black demons did not follow up the attack, but immediately made off, leaving the victim to be found — quite accidentally — by a kanaka, who was looking for horses, and who immediately procured the necessary assistance to carry the wounded man to Peterson's; from whence he was removed to Mr. Gordon's at Scrubby Creek, and thence to hospital. Then a man named John Aldcroft, a late arrival to Herberton from Port Darwin, was travelling towards the Etheridge, and reaching Black Springs this side of the Tate, he was set upon by a party of blacks, one of whose spears entered his back. Drawing the spear from the wound he assumed the offensive by making a rush towards them, upon which they ran, leaving poor Aldcroft master of the field with an ugly flesh wound, from which blood flowed freely. Billy Bice of the New Zealand reef (Georgetown), and another man passed just after the occurrence of the scrimmage, and being armed, which Aldcroft unfortunately was not, they started on the tracks of the attacking party.

---

16   *Brisbane Courier* 29 September 1882 p 2.

Then at Nigger Creek, these troublesome blacks took all the tools from the saw-pits of one of the parties of sawyers, and next morning returned and carried away the iron "dogs" — used for shifting the heavy timber. But "the unkindest cut of all" occurred later on the same day; the men then being at breakfast and within sight of the pits, the blacks came a third time and took away the calico fly and whatever else was left, right from under their eyes. Even this was eclipsed by the doings of a party, who made a raid upon Mr. Philip Garling's camp in the scrub, who not only took away blankets, rations and some comparatively portable tools, but also 'manned' the screw jack, a most ponderous instrument heavily clasped and bolted with iron, which they carried about half-a-mile, where it was subsequently found.[17]

Messrs. Lee and Co were camped near Northcote with a mob of horses, and having been visited by the blacks were induced to provide them with food for some days; one boy remained with them to round up the horses. On 6 November 1882, Mr. Warby of Herberton, and Mr. Gordon, Mr. Lee's partner, were in the neighbourhood and went towards the camp, when they were horror-struck to find Mr. Lee lying on the ground with a wound on his head about four inches long; his neck scratched and cut, his right wrist dislocated, and otherwise injured. He was perfectly insensible, and the two gentlemen lost no time in conveying him to Northcote, where he received all possible aid, and when Mr. Warby left, Lee had recovered his consciousness and felt slightly relieved. However, Mr. Lee had no recollection of what occurred beyond receiving a blow on the head; nor did he see the blacks. Some twelve of them were seen in the early part of the day on the adjacent flats. When Messrs. Warby and Gordon arrived at the

---

17   *Capricornian* 30 September 1882 p 8 & The Week 30 September 1882 p 15.

camp three horses, saddles, bridles, and a blanket had been removed. As Northcote had no police, some six or seven residents rolled up to pursue the miscreants.[18]

The following items were reported from the *Telegraph* of the 21 January 1883:

> We have been informed that several fine horses have been found with spears sticking in them, a short distance from Herberton on the Port Douglas road. Two of the poor brutes died soon after they had been found.[19]

Mr. Egan, a dairyman, accompanied by his son Simon, hired two horses from the firm of Stanfield and Douglas of Herberton, for the purpose of going to Mr. Collins' station to make a purchase of cows with the view to starting a dairy in the neighbourhood of Herberton. It was known that Egan, with his son, passed St. Romans' station on his return with the cattle, and since that time nothing whatever had been seen or heard of them, and fears were raised in the minds of their friends and relatives that something was seriously wrong. Sub-Inspector William Nichols started off with his troopers in search them.[20]

The blacks near Herberton were playing havoc again. A young fellow named Keighran, while out between Nigger and Flaggy Creeks, in search of some of his father's horses, on 5 April 1883, came suddenly on some blacks, who threw three spears at him, but fortunately missed their aim. The young man was happily on horseback, and managed to escape with the loss of his hat. The distance where these blacks were seen was not more than five

---

18   *Capricornian* 25 November 1882 p 19.
19   *Morning Bulletin* 2 February 1883 p 3.
20   *Morning Bulletin* 6 April 1883 p 2.

miles from town.[21]

Christie Palmerston, who was engaged for some time in exploring the northern coast country to find a practicable road from Herberton to the seaboard, had a collision with the blacks. A mob armed with wooden swords attacked him. He shot the chief and made much havoc among the others. He also caught a small boy, who bit and spat at Christie before he allowed himself to be caught. Palmerston further reported that:

> December 27. The boys continued on the main track, and I stopped to gratify my curiosity. There being a fleshy smell arising from an oven, I opened the latter and there saw a female child, half roasted. The skull had been stove in, the whole of the inside cleaned out, and refilled with red-hot stones. The hideous habit of murdering and eating the little girls is carried on far more in these jungles than in any other part of the colonies, which accounts for the female children being so scarce. One of the Mourilyan aborigines informed me that they catch the unsuspecting child by the legs, and dash its head against a tree; also, that picaninny makes quite a delicious meat—he had assisted in eating many.
>
> December 28. Some men armed with swords and shields were coming towards us, commencing, as usual, with frantic action, working themselves into volcanic passion. My boys being dispirited I left them a short distance behind, and met the niggers myself, and the rifle soon made them subside into a more pacific demeanour, and they permitted us to pass. A great quantity of food was lying about their camps, as before described; they had a pair of canvas saddle-bags, some pint pots, pieces of red blankets and tent, and two white cockatoos chattering and walking about the camp. I also saw many human bodies cured like smoked bacon, one very large and quite perfect, excepting the head, the top of which had been severed at the

---

21   *Capricornian* 11 August 1883 p 10 & Queensland Figaro 11 August 1883 p 13.

mouth, and the lower jaw brought down over the chest, its row of white and gaping teeth giving the body a strange aspect. I think the top part of the head is severed from the body because they cannot preserve the brains. The body has rather a withered and greasy appearance, and not a pleasant smell. The one described was in a standing position, with a conical-shaped basket by its side — for the purpose of carrying it, I should imagine. The other bodies were in a doubled position, and jammed into small baskets.[22]

On or about 10 October 1883 at Scrubby Creek, Mr. W.C. Maund's young son, twelve years of age, who was engaged in planting, happened to look up and saw, at about twenty-five to fifty yards distant, a blackfellow aiming a spear at him. The lad made for the house, probably quicker than he had ever run before, but during the run he caught sight of two more blacks approaching under the shade of the fence. The lad then followed his father, whom he pulled up in about three-quarters of a mile down the track, and, when the two returned to the house, they found the three blacks patiently awaiting them at the house, where, by the way, Mrs. Maund was in a delicate state of health. Mr. Maund immediately flew to his gun, when the myalls, dodging from tree to tree, disappeared, but he thought it prudent to fire several shots at a tree in order that the miscreants might see that his aim was sure. After some time, Mr. Maund feeling sure that the blacks would not return, at least on that day, again went on his journey, but, before he had proceeded a quarter of a mile, his son again pulled him up, and informed him that the blacks had returned. They hurried back, when Mr. Maund found his second son keeping the blacks at bay by firing the revolver—the first time he had used such a weapon. Of course, they

---

22 Queenslander 22 September 1883 p 478, 29 September 1883 p 15 & 6 October 1883 p 557.

again disappeared. A party was immediately organised and Mr. C. Hurrey and others searched the surroundings; they heard voices, in the scrub, but thinking that it was Mr. Maund's party, they went on.

The blacks also robbed Glenny's place of all its contents, and, with one of the axes they stole, battered in Walsh's door. Then they robbed Thomas and Garland's place twice, and Mr. Thomas was compelled to remove his family to Cairns. Next, two myalls were discovered in the bed-chambers at Rogan's, and on 26 October, Surveyor Gwynne's kanaka had to apply to Mr. Maund for a rifle to keep the blacks off and, on his return, saw the myalls robbing Garland's camp.[23]

A fatal quarrel took place between two aboriginals at Irvinebank on 2 February 1884. A black known by the name of "Soldier," alias "Policeman," had three gins, to whom "Billy," paid rather marked attention. This annoyed "Policeman," who obtained a Snider rifle by some means, and approaching his rival shot him in the side. The unfortunate victim lingered from eight in the morning till six in the evening, when he died. "Policeman," after shooting Billy, took to the bush, and has not been seen since. It was not positively known how the murderer became possessed of the rifle, but there were certain ugly rumours afloat, which no doubt will be investigated. It was said that he was one of the three blacks who speared Joseph Sculler[24] about two years ago at the Western. Inspector Nichols investigated the matter.[25]

On Sunday 5 August 1884, information was conveyed to the police that a man known as John Conway was missing from the selection of

---

23 *Queensland Times, Ipswich Herald and General Advertiser* 27 October 1883 p 3.
24 Sculler, see page 16 above.
25 *Morning Bulletin* 8 February 1884 p 3

W. McManus on the Russell River, under circumstances which aroused suspicions that he had met with foul play at the hands of the blacks. From the statement furnished to the police by Michael Gallogly, a selector on the Russell, it appeared that Conway was left alone in charge of the selection on 27 July when Barry, the bailiff, left for Herberton.

On 3 August, two men named Ryan and Dillon called at the selection to deliver a message from Barry to Conway but could not find him. They camped the night in the humpy and as Conway did not then appear, they reported the matter at Munro's camp. Gallogly and another man at once went over to Barry's to make a search, and found no blankets or cooked food in the hut, but some flour, tea, sugar, &c., which appeared to be untouched. The fire outside did not appear to have been used for several days. Not finding any trace of Conway, and no black's tracks near the hut, they returned to Munro's camp for further assistance. Mr. Munro and one of his men went back with them and they found one fresh black's track about 200 yards from the hut, in the creek, and apparently made that morning. There were also numerous old blacks' tracks about the creek, but it was known that Barry had a mob of blacks felling scrub for him. Gallogly stated that most of the settlers, among them De Tourris, O'Connell, and himself, were employing blacks but that they had all left their work on the first or second of August, saying they were going to have a big corroboree.

Gallogly was now of opinion that their leaving was connected with the disappearance of Conway. Mr. Munro, who knew Barry's camp pretty well, said three or four scrub knives and some axes and a double-barrelled gun appeared to be missing. No clothes belonging to Conway were left in the hut, but a watch, belt, and pouch, identified as his were found. The settlers in the vicinity feared that the blacks had attacked and killed the missing man in the scrub. The police telegraphed Sub-Inspector Nichols at Herberton, to come down with his native troopers to investigate the matter.[26]

The mystery surrounding the disappearance of John Conway from McManus' selection on the Russell River was cleared away by information obtained by Mr. Mackey, a selector on that river, which left little doubt that Conway was murdered by the blacks. Mr. Mackey reported that he had captured a black boy, known to the settlers by the name of Sandy, who, after being detained for over a day, confessed that "blackfellow Paddy killed white fellow," meaning Conway. An aboriginal called Paddy was known to have been working at times for Conway. On the information furnished by Sandy, Mr. Mackey, in company with another man and Sandy, proceeded to search for the body; but without success, and as the boy Sandy managed to make his escape from them, the chance of finding the body of the unfortunate man in the dense scrub that abounds in this part appeared remote.[27]

On 10 August 1884, Sub-Inspector Carr and five native troopers arrived in Cairns, and on 12 August proceeded to the Russell to assist in the search.[28] On 17 August, Sub-Inspector Carr returned to Cairns after an absence of six days, and reported that he had found the remains of Conway, the missing man, and that from the marks on the body the deceased had evidently been stoned to death. After burying the remains, he continued his investigations and was able to trace the deed to four aboriginals who were well known.

---

26 *Cairns Post* 7 August 1884 p 2.
27 *Cairns Post* 14 August 1884 p 3.
28 *Cairns Post* 14 August 1884 p 3.

The four blacks concerned in the crime fled to the hills, but were expected to be captured before long. The reason for the crime was partly traceable to revenge for treatment received at the hands of Conway, who had been cautioned by some of the settlers in the district to be more circumspect in his dealings with the blacks, but he heeded not the advice, and had paid the penalty of his rashness with his life.[29]

Then the blacks, on 17 September, speared a man named John Wild, a miner, in the arm while lying in his bunk, and robbed his hut. It was only on 17 September that Sub-Inspector William Nichols and his troopers had left for Highfields where the blacks were also been making depredations. They also robbed several settlers at Scrubby Creek.[30]

Sam, a blackboy residing in Herberton, decided on visiting the camp of his friends at Newellton. He accordingly borrowed his masters' horse and rode out, and shortly after arrival amongst them received a spear through the muscle of his arm. Sam was reticent upon the subject of the casus belli, but from the tenor of his remarks it was inferred that there was a lady in the case. He broke off the spear close to the wound and left a piece sticking in which stopped the bleeding somewhat.[31]

On September 24, 1884, the Commissioner of Police received information from the Walsh River that two men named Morgan and Bailey had been murdered, their skulls being smashed by their two blackboys, who then cleared out with their horses, saddles, and other articles. The murderers belonged to the Tate tribe and were identified.[32]

---

29 *Cairns Post* 21 August 1884 p 3.
30 *Cairns Post* 18 September 1884 p 3.
31 *Morning Bulletin* 15 November 1883 p 3.
32 *Capricornian* 27 September 1884 p 1.

IRVINEBANK

Late October 1884, Sergeant Breene, of Herberton, wired Inspector Isley of Port Douglas that information had been received that the bodies of seven aboriginals, supposed to have been murdered, had been found near Irvinebank, about twenty-five miles from Herberton. The police were making inquiries.[33]

Late on Christmas Eve 1884, a painful feeling of anxiety was created in Cairns by the news brought in from the Mulgrave River by Donald Shaw that Donald McAulay, a selector on that river had fallen a victim to the treachery of the blacks. Shaw, who was working on McAulay's selection, reported the matter to the police. After some difficulty, McAulay's mutilated body was taken to McPherson's camp, where it was buried. Two blacks called Tommy and Sambo, who had confessed to knowing about the murder were taken to Cairns. These boys say that McAulay was killed by two blacks called Charley Daylight and Jimmy Barlow, and a piccaninny, which appears to be most probably the truth, as they were the blacks which were in the canoe that McAulay went up river in. Charley Daylight and one of the boys, Tommy, were in custody suspected of being concerned in the murder of Conway on the Russell River in July last. The most revolting circumstance in connection with this horrible murder was the discovery of the body minus some of its members, which leaves little doubt that after killing their victim, the murderers indulged in their well-known cannibalistic tastes on McAulay's body.[34]

---

33 *Morning Bulletin* 31 October 1884 p 5.
34 *Cairns Post* 1 January 1885 p 2.

THE IRVINEBANK MASSACRE

MAGISTERIAL ENQUIRY INTO THE DEATH OF DONALD McAULAY December 30. (Before R. T. Hartley, G. Adams, R. A. Kingsford, and R. J. Gorton, Esqs. J.J.P.)

Thomas Ryan was the first witness called, and deposed: I am a contractor residing on deceased's selection. I knew Donald McAulay. He was a selector residing on the Mulgrave River. I last saw him on Sunday, 21 December 1884, about 7.30 a.m. He left the camp that morning for McPherson's selection in a blackfellow's canoe, accompanied by two blackfellows named Charley Daylight and Tommy. I saw them start, and about an hour afterwards Tommy returned to the camp on foot. I asked him what he had done with the canoe, and he said that another blackfellow had taken his place in it, and it had gone on. Next day Tommy came back again, and I asked him what had become of the white fellow and canoe. He said white fellow left canoe at Yarramaburra, meaning McPherson's selection, and went along the track to town. This was on 22 December, and I became uneasy that McAulay did not return, and had my suspicions aroused that he had met with foul play. On 23 December two blacks came in a canoe, and were very impudent, and two more came on the opposite side of the inlet armed with spears, which was very unusual. When they saw I was armed they went behind the mangrove. When Shaw came home to dinner, I told him the particulars of what had happened, and he agreed to go with me in search of McAulay on the following day. On 24 December, Donald Shaw and myself started up river, and had not gone above three-quarters of a mile when we came upon the canoe that McAulay left in. We went ashore and saw two blackfellows, one of them Tommy, whom we took into the boat and proceeded up river. About a quarter of a mile further on we saw Charley Daylight on the bank. As we passed, he called to the blacks in the boat in broken English to know if we had firearms, and when they told him we had he bolted up the bank and called out to those in the boat to leave us. This we prevented them doing, and went onto McPherson's, but finding McAulay had not been there we proceeded to Mr. Adams', where Shaw got a horse and came into town to report the matter to the police. When we went ashore at McPherson's we rolled our firearms in mackintosh, owing to the rain, and put them under a sheet of iron, but whilst we were there the two blacks cleared out, and our firearms disappeared with them. On 25 December, Shaw returned with Constable Portley and a black tracker. We remained that day at McPherson's, expecting the blacks to come into camp again. Next morning two blacks, Tommy and Sambo, now in Court, came to the camp. We detained them, and Shaw, Constable Portley, McKay, myself, a kanaka, and three blacks went down the river in the boat. After we had proceeded about a mile, we discovered the dead body of McAulay in the river, and towed it to a sandspit. When we found the body, the head was nearly severed from the trunk, the entrails were out, and one leg was missing. When the blacks saw the body, they tried to escape; Tommy succeeded, but was afterwards recaptured. We took the body back to McPherson's, and had it buried next day. The two boys that went in the canoe with McAulay were aboriginal natives of the Mulgrave River. McAulay never did any harm to the blacks, but always treated them very kindly. There are no gins about the camp on the Mulgrave. About three weeks ago I travelled down the Mulgrave with Charley Daylight, and he seemed quite inoffensive. I could not recognise the features of the body as those of McAulay, they being so decomposed.

By the Bench: The blacks were in the habit of coming to the selection with fish, but were not allowed to remain about the place for long. Charley Daylight was one of the most civilised blacks on the river. McAulay had no firearms with him. We requested him to take some, but he would not.

Donald Shaw deposed: I am a bushman engaged on McAulay's selection. I heard the evidence given by the previous witness, the particulars of which as stated by him are correct.

Alexander McKay deposed: I am a selector operating on the Mulgrave River. I last saw deceased about three weeks ago. I remember Shaw and Ryan coming to my selection on Wednesday 24 December and enquiring for McAulay. On learning he had not been there they left for Mr. Adams' to report the matter. On 25 December, Shaw, Ryan, the constable, and tracker returned, and on the 30th I went down the river with them and the two black boys (in Court) and my kanaka, in search of McAulay. We found the dead body of McAulay lying on the fork of a tree partly in the water. The left leg and left arm were cut off, and the head was almost severed from the body. We had to get a bag to remove the body. My kanaka first drew attention to the body, and one of the blacks wanted to make believe it was an alligator, and both were evidently anxious to pass it by. When we would go to it, they exhibited great fear. They both tried to escape, and Tommy did so. We took the body back with us, and interred it at my place on Saturday. The body was too decomposed for me to recognise it as McAulay's, but I am convinced that it was his. I have known deceased twenty years. To the best of my knowledge he has always been kind to the blacks. As a rule, the gins do not come into the camp. The deceased was, I think, about 55 to 60 years of age, and leaves a wife and family residing on the Clarence River, N.S.W.

By the Bench: I believe that deceased was murdered by the blacks. Witness then made a statement to the effect that he believed one of the blacks then in Court named Tommy and Charley Daylight were the murderers of John Conway[35] a few months back off the Russell River. His reason for this suspicion was that these two blacks had come on to the Mulgrave about the time of the murder with new shirts on, which had not been given them so far as he could ascertain by any of the white people.

Constable Portley gave corroborative evidence, adding that before anything respecting the death of McAulay had been said to the blacks, Tommy and Sambo, they said it was Charley Daylight and Jimmy Barlow who had done it. On being questioned by the Bench, witness said he did not know if the boys in Court had anything to

---

35 See pages 25-28 above.

do with the death of deceased, but they seemed to know all about it.

This concluded the evidence, which will be forwarded in due course to the Attorney-General. The evidence of the aboriginals, although an interpreter was present, was not taken in case they should prove to be parties to the crime.[36]

---

36 *Cairns Post* 1 January 1885 p 2.

2

Police Presence

It was found necessary to increase the police force in consequence of the extension of mining activities in the North. The great tin deposits in the Cook district were attracting populations. On the Wild River, there were between 400 and 500 miners, and the scene of their activity had been named Herberton.[37]

The report of the Commissioner of Police for 1881 presented to Parliament on 4 July 1882, noted that during the year, eleven new police stations had been formed—including, Herberton.

---

37 Queenslander 5 February 1881 p 165.

Cook Sub-Division D: Port Douglas 1881[38]

Police Stations	Officers	NCOs & Constables	Native Troopers
Port Douglas	1	9	7
Barron River	1	1	11
Cairns		3	
Herberton		4	
Kingsborough		1	
Thornborough		3	1

On 20 May 1881, Courts of Petty Sessions were established at Herberton and Constable Joseph F. Delaney was appointed Acting Clerk of Petty Sessions at Herberton with effect from 1 June 1881.[39]

On or about 25 February 1882, Sub-Inspector Alexander Douglas Douglas was transferred from Brisbane to Herberton, to take charge of the white police at Herberton.[40]

In July of 1882, W M Mowbray was appointed police magistrate at Herberton, in place of P W Pears, who was transferred; W M Mowbray was also appointed mineral land commissioner at Herberton.[41]

The murder of John Skene by blacks at Nigger Creek so outraged the residents of Herberton and surrounds that a petition was sent to Mr T McIlwraith, the Premier on 3 April 1882.[42] It contained 217 signatures. This petition sought the introduction of Native Police patrols into the Wild River district as a deterrent to aboriginal attacks on white residents.

---

38 Report of Commissioner of Police 1881, dated 19 June 1882, Table A.
39 GG Vol. XXVIII] 21 May 1881 [No. 66 p 1240.
40 The Week 25 February 1882 p 7. Douglas returned to Brisbane on or about 22 June, Brisbane Courier 23 June 1882 p 2.
41 *Brisbane Courier* 15 July 1882 p 5.
42 See pages 17 and 18 above.

On about 14 November 1882, 1st class Sub-Inspector William Nichols of Native Police reported to Herberton for duty.[43] The Native Police camp was stationed a few miles from Herberton at Nigger Creek.

Cook Sub-Division D: Port Douglas 1883[44]

Police Stations	Officers	NCOs & Constables	Native Troopers
Port Douglas	1	9	2
Barron River	1	1	10
Cairns		4	
Herberton		6	
Kingsborough		1	
Nigger Creek	1	1	7
Thornborough		3	1
Watsonville		2	

Mr. Seymour, Commissioner of Police, accompanied by Sub-Inspector Carr, arrived in Herberton on 7 May 1883 and left on 9 May. He also visited Watsonville. Of course, he made no comment on the localities he visited.[45] In early 1884, a reserve of 640 acres was set aside for a police paddock on Nigger Creek, county of Cardwell, parish of Herberton.[46]

Nichols was not happy with his posting. On 6 December 1882, he wrote to Inspector Isley at Port Douglas as follows:

> I have the honour to apply for three months leave of absence. I may point out to you that for the last six years I have been stationed in outside districts and that I have only had three weeks leave during the time I have been in the police force. During the last three months I

---

43 Promoted 1st Class Sub-Inspector 1 July 1882, Qld PG Vol. XIX.] 5 August 1882 [No. 16, p 132.
44 Report of Commissioner of Police 1883, dated 6 August 1884, Table A.
45 The Week 26 May 1883 p 6.
46 *Telegraph* 4 February 1884 Page 5.

have had particularly heavy duty to perform having been continually in the saddle without hardly a day's respite.[47]

Nichols had come from the Oak Park Native Police camp which was about forty miles from Gilberton, in the Etheridge goldfield district. He had taken over the camp from Sub-Inspector M. T. Day on 21 May 1880. Nichols brought with him to the Nigger Creek camp, constable J Stewart[48] and native troopers Sambo, Sandy, Pituri, Larry and Carlo. He also had the services of another white camp constable G McInerney.[49] It may also come as a bit of a surprise to know that Nichols completed the establishment of the camp with 6 gins and twelve horses. The Day Journal at Oak Park described the gins as "general useful." Perhaps the most significant and traumatic event in Nichols' recent service history was his presence at the spearing to death of Sub-Inspector Harold Pollock Kaye by the blacks at Woolgar on 14 September 1881.

Isley wrote to the Commissioner of Police as follows:

> Sub-Inspector Nichols has only lately arrived at Herberton with his detachment to form a new station there. If a competent officer can be sent to replace him and superintend the erection of buildings etc, I cannot object to his application; otherwise I would wish the leave to be deferred. I do not doubt that Mr Nichols has earned his leave and would strongly recommend it under different circumstances.[50]

Commissioner DT Seymour's decision was, "Inform Inspector Isley that

---

47 QSA ID564169, Nichols' staff file.
48 Details: 317 John Stewart, sworn in 29 July 1880. Qld Police Book of Names 1864-1974. Joined Nichols at Oak Park NP camp on 20 March 1882, QSA ID86147.
49 Details: 548 George McInerney, sworn in 12 April 1883. Qld Police Book of Names 1864-1974. When McInerney joined Nigger Creek NP camp is unknown.
50 QSA ID564169.

Sub-Inspector Nichols will be shortly relieved and transferred to Brisbane, D.T.S. 3/1/83."

Nichols service at Nigger Creek was not a happy time. On 31 July 1884, Isley wrote to Nichols regarding his failure to lodge his June 1884 returns and vouchers after having warned him that the items were to be in Isley's office by 23 July. Moreover, what returns and vouchers Nichols had sent in contained errors or were incomplete. As a consequence, Isley duly wrote to the Commissioner setting out his transgressions chapter and verse. To wit, Nichols was neglectful and carelessness in failing to comply with his duty to furnish Isley with the relevant returns and vouchers. The Commissioner's response was, "Sub-Inspector Nichols' pay must be withheld when his returns are in arrears, D.T.S. 18/8/84."

Nichols, in turn, advised the Commissioner that he had not failed to send in the necessary forms and vouchers. They had been delayed because he had been ordered to patrol the Russell River (sixty miles south of Cairns) which had taken three to four weeks and further that he had been unwell with fever and would provide a doctor's certificate to that effect. Dr Bowkett's certificate dated 28 August 1884 duly stated Nichols had been ill of malarial fever for the last 10 days and unable to attend duties. Nichols also asked for a transfer to another outside district.[51]

Then all hell broke loose, when the following appeared in the Press:

> Considerable dissatisfaction has been expressed at Irvinebank during the past week with regard to the slaughter of some aboriginals at that place by the native police. The facts, so far as I have been able to ascertain, are as follows: The Sub-Inspector of Native Police

---

[51] QSA ID564169.

obtained from a local J. P. a warrant for the arrest of two aboriginals at Irvinebank, whom he had reason to suspect were implicated in the murder of Morgan and Bailey on the Walsh. On arriving at Irvinebank, the warrants were produced and the men arrested. A day or so afterwards, the bodies of two males, two gins and a piccaninny were found within a mile and a half of the township. Death had evidently been caused by rifle shots; the gash made by a Snider bullet needs no searching for, and was too visible to leave any doubt. As one of the males had never left the township for months, and the gins and piccaninny were recognised immediately, it was determined to have an inquiry into the matter. Mr. Mowbray, our P.M., was sent for, but was at Thornborough on duty. On his return, however, he went out to hold the inquiry, taking with him Dr. Bowkett. The place where the bodies were found was visited, but only a few charred bones remained to tell the tale, every other vestige of the five bodies having disappeared. This daring act has given the affair another start, and an angry feeling is prevalent against those who are endeavouring to shield the perpetrators of this cruel act by removing all traces of the deed.[52]

Thus, began the saga of, "Who killed the Aborigines?"

---

52 *Morning Bulletin* 31 October 1884 p 5.

3

Inquest

The *Herberton Advertiser* of 15 November 1884 published the report of the magisterial enquiry into the Irvinebank aboriginal murders:

> A magisterial enquiry touching the cause of death of certain aboriginals near Irvinebank, on or about the 18th October, was commenced at Irvinebank on the 23rd October 1884.
>
> George William Seaman deposed that he was a clerk in the employ of John Moffat and Co., at Irvinebank. On Wednesday, the 15th October, he saw black troopers riding about and the blacks staying in the camp scattered in all directions. He went down to the township, and on the allotment near Bethel's saw a blackfellow known as Spoopendyke handcuffed and, with his feet tied together, fastened to a fence. Spoopendyke was swearing out loud. There was a black trooper in charge of him. Sub-Inspector Nichols was also there. Shortly afterwards the troopers led Spoopendyke away fastened between two horses. He ran up to Mr. Moffat's residence to acquaint him of the matter, and on looking down saw another black boy, named Toby, being led away by a trooper, and, he thought, Mr. Carr's Cadet. He was taken along the track towards Herberton. On Friday, the 17th October, he saw the troopers out again; they camped

on a creek, and were walking about all the afternoon. He saw some of the troopers on Saturday. Mr. Nichols and another were about during the day, the troopers were absent. At nightfall he noticed one of the troopers bringing five or six horses with saddles on into the camp. About 8 o'clock on the same night a man named Sedgewick told witness (Seaman) that he had heard five or six rifle shots fired. On the Sunday morning following, a blackfellow named Alicky told witness that he had been with the troopers to a blacks' camp where two gins, a piccaninny and a blackfellow were shot or otherwise killed by the troopers. After breakfast Messrs, Jno. Moffat, Peter Moffat, Linedale, Dineen and witness were piloted by Alicky to a camp where they saw the remains of two gins, a piccaninny and a blackfellow. The blackfellow was known in the camp as King Billy. He had been about the Silver Camp and Irvinebank for months past. Witness also recognised the body of one of the gins, who was in the habit of knocking about Tait's public-house. The bodies were all partially burned. One gin was unrecognisable, but there was sufficient of the remains to show that there had been two gins and a piccaninny. The lower extremities were destroyed by fire. The bodies appeared to have been drawn together; some logs and bushes piled on them and then set fire to. Witness noticed bullet marks on two or three trees in the vicinity and out of one of them extracted the bullet produced. He found one of the pairs of handcuffs, produced, about 200 yards from the bodies, and found the other pair, produced, close to the bodies. The cartridge case, also produced, was within a few feet of them. He found a woomera and spear close to the tree from which the bullet was extracted. Also found a shield, partially burned, lying close to the bodies. On the 22nd October witness went up to the camp in company with Constable Moroney. The bodies were much more burned and very much decomposed. The fire was burning when he first saw the bodies, but was not burning when seen in company with constable Moroney. On the 23rd October he visited the spot where the bodies were lying and found a heap of ashes and the fire burning. When first the bodies were seen they had not been dead more than 12 or 14 hours. He had seen one of gins on the previous day at Tait's

INQUEST

public-house. He did not take notice of any wounds, but fancied the head of one of the gins had been smashed in. Around the camp were pieces of old blankets, such as were distributed to the blacks. Believed the name of one of the gins was Kitty, and knew that she was the mother of a black boy, Tait has with his pack horses. Mr. John Moffat also gave evidence which corroborated that of the previous witness in every particular. The enquiry was then adjourned.

The adjourned enquiry was resumed at Herberton, on 1st November.

Constable Moroney deposed that on the 22nd October he visited the scene of the reported murder of the blacks, near Irvinebank, and had seen something like the remains of four aboriginals, partly destroyed by fire. He visited the place next day in company with Dr. Bowkett, Mr. Moffat, Mr. Seaman and Sergeant Breene, when he saw nothing but a heap of ashes.

Dr. Bowkett deposed that he accompanied the Police Magistrate and others to a hill about two miles from Irvinebank, and was there shown a heap of ashes, still smouldering. Was informed that human bodies had been burnt there. Examined the heap and found some small bone, but was unable to identify them as human bones, they being so much charred.

The enquiry was further adjourned.

The hearing of the enquiry was continued at Irvinebank on the 12th November. J. C. Sedgewick deposed that he heard shots fired on Saturday evening, and had an idea what the shooting was for.

Alessandro Leoni deposed that he heard shots fired and heard screams. He afterwards saw the dead bodies of four aboriginals.

The enquiry then terminated, and the evidence forwarded to the Attorney-General.[53]

---

53 *Cairns Post* 20 November 1884 p 2; *Brisbane Courier* 12 December 1884 p 5; *Telegraph* 13 December 1884 p 4; The Week 20 December 1884 p 22 & *Queenslander* 20 December 1884 p 992 & QSA ID348709 JUS/N110/511.

THE IRVINEBANK MASSACRE

Certificate of Particulars of Inquest

Headings	Particulars
Found	Near Irvinebank 19 October 1884
Date of death	18 October 1884
Supposed cause of death	Killed by troopers of Nigger Creek NP detachment.
Persons last seen in company of deceased	No evidence
Names of suspected persons	NP detachment then at Irvinebank
Accused	None
Names of witnesses	George William Seaman, John Moffat JP, Denis Moroney, WB Bowkett, Alessandro Leoni
Suspicious circumstances	Native Troopers seen and report of firearms heard in vicinity on 18 October 1884. Discovery of bodies partially destroyed by fire on 19 October; bodies subsequently destroyed by fire.

On 14 November 1884, Police Magistrate Mowbray at Herberton posted the depositions to the Attorney-General and wrote as follows:

> I again adjourned it until the arrival at Herberton of Inspector Isley; accompanied by him I revisited Irvinebank and took further evidence on the 12th instant; I attempted at this time to examine the aboriginal Alick, whose evidence should be the most important but was unable to obtain any intelligible statement from him. The exhibitions which I now forward under separate cover, for your consideration, disclose clear circumstantial evidence of the outrage having been perpetrated by native troopers who were then patrolling the neighbourhood under the charge of Sub-Inspector Nichols. Inspector Isley informs me that Mr Nichols has in the meantime been suspended from office.[54]

---

54   QSA ID348709.

The Attorney-General noted the following on the cover sheet of the depositions:

> To Colonial Secretary: It is pretty clear from the depositions that four aboriginals have been barbarously murdered by native troopers. It might not be impossible for the police by further inquiries to establish the identity of some of the offenders. AR (Arthur Rutledge) 29/11/84.

The Colonial Secretary sent the depositions to the Commissioner of Police who noted, "I have directed the dismissal of all troopers and Nichols has been dismissed. I do not see much chance of success in a prosecution. Seymour 2.12.84."

Arising out of the above inquiry, Inspector Isley requested Nichols to attend the Herberton police station for purpose of Isley placing before Nichols such portions of the evidence as related to the troopers for his explanation? On 14 November 1884, Nichols explained that he knew nothing about these blacks (the deceased) and he was convinced his troopers would not shoot women and children. However, he admitted that the troopers were out of camp late on 18 October 1884. Isley was not satisfied with Nichols explanation and Nichols was suspended with effect 15 November 1884.

The actual sequence of events is revealed in the Day Journal of the Nigger Creek NP camp.

THE IRVINEBANK MASSACRE

Day Journal of the Nigger Creek NP camp.[55]

Date	Tprs in Camp	Gins in Camp	Horses	Occurrences
15/11/1884				15th Sub-Insp Nichols being suspended from duty Mr Cadet Garraway will take charge of detachment on his arrival. As all the books and records of the station are in arrears, Mr Garraway will not take on full charge until everything is made up to his satisfaction. Upon which he will advise me by wire. Sub-Insp Nichols will proceed to Port Douglas to await further instructions, taking orderly and 3 horses. Signed Isley Inspector
18/11/1884				Handed over Nigger Creek Detachment to Cadet Sub-Insp Garraway 18 Nov 1884. sgnd W Nichols Sub-Insp, Roland Garraway Cadet Sub-Insp.
18/11/1884	5	5	22	Sub-Inspector Nichols started at 10 am on horse Tom Brown also trooper Sandy on horse Monarch & pack horse Burnes.

On 28 November 1884, the Commissioner of Police was advised by the Colonial Secretary that the Governor in Council had dismissed William Nichols from the police force with effect 15 November 1884.[56] The Government also dismissed the black troopers concerned in the raid on the blacks at Irvinebank.[57]

---

55 QSA ID86147.
56 1st Class Wm. Nichols dismissed 15 November 1884, Qld PG VOL. XXI.] 6 December 1884 [No. 25. p 257.
57 Cairns Post 11 December 1884 p 2.

4

Committal Proceedings

Generally speaking, in the English criminal justice system, the following procedure is adopted: when information of a crime is given to police, they investigate the matter and, if persuaded that a crime has been committed, arrest the suspect and take him before a court to be tried. Where the suspect is alleged to have committed a serious crime such as murder, the suspect is entitled to go before a magistrate who will determine if there is sufficient prima facie evidence such that a properly instructed jury could find the person guilty of the charge. This preliminary hearing of police evidence is known as committal proceedings. At no stage in these proceedings is the defendant required to enter a plea and he is permitted to cross-examine the police witnesses. If the magistrate is satisfied there is a prima facie case against the defendant, then he will commit the defendant to the next sittings of a superior court to be tried by a judge and jury. In the case of murder, the defendant is usually remanded into custody awaiting trial.

It seems that a decision was made by A L Morisset, Inspector at Townsville to place John E Barry, 1st Class Detective on special duty to investigate the murder of the Irvinebank Aborigines. On 3 January 1885, Barry arrested William Nichols at Port Douglas on a charge of being an accessory before the fact to the murder by his black troopers at Irvinebank on eighteenth October 1884 of the deceased Aborigines. On 11 January 1885, Barry arrested the six troopers (four from Nigger Creek and two from Barron River) at Herberton on a charge of murder to wit, causing the death of certain Aborigines at Irvinebank on eighteenth October 1884.

Now it is to be assumed that Barry had a copy of the depositions from the inquest into the deaths of the Irvinebank Aborigines prior to the arrest of the above suspects, but he didn't have statements from two very relevant witnesses namely, Roland Garraway and Constable John Stewart. According to Isley, in a telegram to the Commissioner of 19 January 1885, Barry 'reported Cadet Garraway for not having his statement written on Barry's first interview with Garraway; Barry (also) bounced him telling him he was putting (sic) much in same position as Nichols. Garraway then declined to make a statement but will answer any questions in the witness box. Const Stewart the camp keeper also bounced by Barry and declined to make written statement.' Isley also informed the Commissioner that he supported Garraway and Stewart and would not order them to make written statements and that Barry could take notes whilst interviewing them.[58] Nichols' committal was held separate from the committal of the

---

58 QSA ID564169.

troopers.

Regina v. William Nichols

The committal proceedings were held at the Court House, Herberton before the police magistrate, W. M. Mowbray on 21 January 1885. The preliminary matters such as proof of arrest and that the defendant admitted he was William Nichols was given in evidence by Barry. The charge read:

> On suspicion of being an accessory before the fact to the murder by **his** black troopers at Irvinebank on the eighteenth of October last of a male aboriginal known as "King Billy" of a female aboriginal known as "Kitty" of another female aboriginal name unknown and an aboriginal piccaninny name unknown.

Plunkett's Australian Magistrate [1866] defined an accessory before the fact as one who, being absent at the time of felony committed, procures, commands, or counsels another to commit a crime.

The first witness called to go to the proof of the crime charged against Nichols was Roland Walter Garraway:

> On the fifteenth of October last (1884), I was stationed at Barron River Camp. On the sixteenth of October last I went to the Nigger Creek Camp. I saw the accused (Nichols) there. He was Sub-Inspector of police in charge of Nigger Creek Police Camp.
>
> Five of the troopers who were brought before the Court yesterday on a charge of murder were in his detachment on that occasion. Their names were Sambo, Sandy, Pituri, Larry and Carlo. The other two accused who were before the Court yesterday on the same charge were in my detachment. Their names were Willie and Jimmey. On the sixteenth of October last the accused told me that he was shorthanded and would I lend him the assistance of myself, troopers and horses.

I replied that I was under Sub-Inspector Carr's instructions and I could not deviate from them without the consent of Inspector Isley. A Sub-Inspector of police is a higher rank than a cadet. Accused then told me to wire to Inspector Isley for instructions. I did so on the seventeenth of October. I received a telegram from Inspector Isley. In consequence of that telegram, I put myself and troopers under Sub-Inspector Nichols.

I know Irvinebank. All the accused (Troopers) I identified yesterday went with Sub-Inspector Nichols and me to Irvinebank on the seventeenth of October. We camped at Irvinebank that night.

On the morning of the eighteenth Sub-Inspector Nichols told me to send my troopers with his on patrol. I did so. To the best of my belief seven troopers went on patrol that morning. One stayed at the camp. The seven who went, went on horseback. They were all armed to the best of my belief.

I look at exhibit 1. They were armed with a rifle and a cartridge belt. I cannot say about the handcuffs. The trooper who stayed at the camp was Sandy. The troopers were dressed in ordinary uniform. They started between nine and ten o'clock in the morning. They returned between nine and ten o'clock p.m. The horses were brought to the camp about sundown. Charlie the trooper brought the horses to camp. The troopers were roughly paraded before leaving the camp that morning by Sub-Inspector Nichols. I heard him tell the troopers, "Catch Tommy and mind you don't use your rifles." Those are as nearly the exact words as I can remember. I believe it was impossible for Sub-Inspector Nichols to have given any other order without my hearing it. I was close by him the whole morning up to the time the troopers left the camp. Sub-Inspector Nichols did not go in charge of the troopers that day. He did not send me in charge of them. I should say it was not his duty to go with the troopers himself when they are sent scouting like that or to have sent me in charge of the troopers. I was about the camp all day on the eighteenth of October last.

I am aware the troopers who were on patrol on the eighteenth of October last are under remand. I do not know that it was wilful neglect of duty on Sub-Inspector Nichols part in not going with the troopers on that day. I do not consider there was any neglect of duty on the part of Sub-Inspector Nichols on that day. I have been in the Native Police force since June 1884.

On the nineteenth of October I returned to Herberton. Mr Nichols and all the troopers went to Nigger Creek. Mr Nichols has since left the police. Before doing so he handed me all government property in his possession including firearms and handcuffs.

I refer to exhibit 2 and to the October Pay Sheet for Nigger Creek. I believe it is in Mr Nichols handwriting. The names of the troopers are Corporal Sambo, Troopers Sandy, Carlo, Pituri and Joe. Joe and Larry, the troopers before the Court yesterday are identical. Those are the names of the troopers who formed Mr Nichols detachment in October last.

I look at exhibit 3. They correspond with the handcuffs used by any police. I look at exhibit 4. Detective Barry and I extracted two bullets from two cartridges on Monday last. They correspond with the cartridges used by the troopers excepting in not having a bullet in them. I look at exhibit 5. They correspond in appearance with the first two examined by me.

There were no other Native Police officers at Irvinebank on the eighteenth of October last beside Sub-Inspector Nichols and myself. I returned to the Baron River on the twenty-first of October from Herberton. I did not hear of the murders at Irvinebank before leaving Herberton on the twenty-first of October. I left Herberton about a quarter to eleven in the forenoon. I saw Mr Nichols I believe a few minutes before I left. I do not know that Sub-Inspector Nichols had been to Irvinebank between the nineteenth and twenty-first of October.

Cross-examined by accused, Nichols: I remember the words you made use of to the troopers on the morning of the eighteenth of

October. You said, "Catch Tommy and mind you don't use your rifles." The boys then left the camp at once. None of those boys returned during that day. You could have had no opportunity of seeing them without my knowing it. I first noticed the boys when they returned. I called out to you, "Oh, the boys are here." You spoke to Sambo in presence of the other boys. I think you said, "You been bringing in Tommy, Sambo?" He replied, "No catch em marme, think em gone away." The first I heard of the murders was from a telegram in the papers. If you had heard it about Irvinebank, I think I should have heard it too. If you had gone to Irvinebank between the nineteenth and twenty-first of October, I should have known it.

Re-examined by Detective Barry: I went to the store at Irvinebank on the eighteenth of October. There is a bit of a ridge between the store and the place where we were camped that day. The camp cannot be seen from the store. I was at the store several times which time do you mean? Mr Nichols was not with me every time I was at the store. He might have been with me half a dozen times. I may have been twice to the store without Nichols. I saw on one occasion when I returned from the store Alicky, an aboriginal and a gin talking with Mr Nichols. Mr Nichols could not have sent a message by Sandy to the troopers during my absence. I believe Mr Nichols could not have seen any of the troopers who might have returned to the camp during my absence at the store. Sandy, the trooper, Alicky and the gin left Mr Nichols and went away together. On going away, Mr Nichols said to them, "Alicky know where some spears are, suppose you find em you bring em in."

Before I returned from the store Sub-Inspector Nichols could not have given other instructions to Sandy. They were not within ten or twelve yards of Mr Nichols when I came back to camp and I heard him call out to them. They had not reached the camp. Sandy, Alicky and the gin went away about five o'clock in the evening. Sandy returned that night between half past eight and ten o'clock.

Examined by the Bench: When I returned to the camp, I saw the spears lying beside the gin and Sandy standing alongside the spears. Trooper Charlie a deserter returned with the horses about sundown but none of the other troopers returned before half past eight or ten o'clock. I was at the store with accused for rations and forage on the evening of the seventeenth. Alicky came of his own free will to the camp. Mr Nichols sent me to the store to see if Alicky was coming or not and to get some stores. The gin I saw standing by the spears at eight was the same gin I saw with Alicky in the afternoon. Mr Nichols told me that his wish to get Tommy was to obtain some information from him about some murders I believe. He said Tommy was a runner between tribes. When trooper Charlie returned, he said Sambo had sent him back with the horses the country was too rough. I asked him where the boys were; I think he said they had gone to Return Creek. I am not sure. Sgnd Roland W Garraway dated 21 January 1885, on oath at Herberton before WM Mowbray PM.[59]

The next witness called was James Bethel who ran the Mining Exchange hotel at Irvinebank. Bethel stated that he heard about the murders on a Sunday but could not remember the date and that Nichols had come to his hotel on the day before to speak to Alicky about where Spoopendyke's spears were and that Nichols and Alicky had walked off towards the camp about 4 or 5 o'clock in the afternoon. Under cross-examination by Nichols, Bethel stated that Nichols was in his hotel about 7 or 8 o'clock on Saturday night, 18 October last and that Alicky left with him. Bethel also placed Nichols in his hotel on the morning of 19 October as he was on his way to Herberton. Bethel was also examined by Barry about the fact that a summons had been served on Alicky for his appearance at these proceeding and that Alicky had failed to appear.

The final witness was John Bacey Isley who stated, "In sending out

---

59 QSA ID847145.

scouts it is not customary for the officer to go. Patrolling is when all the detachment is working together. I consider it to have been an error in judgement to send out so large a party of troopers without an officer in charge of them and not a neglect of duty."

Detective Barry then closed his case and stated that he had no evidence to refute that given by Cadet Garraway. The Police Magistrate said that no neglect of duty would make a man accessory to a felony; neglect of duty would make a him amenable to a charge of manslaughter; but that would not stand in this case as other prisoner were under committal for the murder; and, where a charge of murder was sustained against anyone no one could be charged with manslaughter in connection with the same crime. Lord Hale's definition of an accessory before the fact was as follows: An accessory before the fact is one who, being absent at the time of the offence committed, does yet procure, counsel, command, or abet another to commit a felony; the bare concealment of a felony to be committed will not make the party concealing it an accessory before the fact.[60] Mr Mowbray P.M. then discharged William Nichols.

On 21 January 1885, Barry wired OIC Detectives, Brisbane, "Nichols discharged, done best I could with most unwilling witnesses, expect leave for Townsville tomorrow via Cairns."

Isley also wired the Commissioner as follows on 21 January 1885:

> Re Irvinebank charge against ex Sub-Inspector Nichols fell through, Cadet Garraway's evidence was to the effect that Nichols gave the troopers orders when sending them out scouting on no account to use their rifles. I was also a witness; copies of deposition will be

---

60   *Herberton Advertiser* 24 January 1885 Vol. 5 No. 7 & QSA ID847145.

forwarded soon as possible.

Given the above legal definition of an accessary before the fact, the dismissal of the charge against Nichols is not surprising. On the face it, Barry was attempting to hold Nichols responsible for the actions of the troopers, by framing the charge as follows: "being an accessary before the fact to the murder by **his** black troopers at Irvinebank". In other words, Barry was alleging Nichols was criminally liable simple because he was in command of the troopers. Barry failed to realise that he had to prove that Nichols had to have done something or failed to do something in connection with the murder, simply being in command was not enough. In this case, the evidence was that Nichols had instructed the troopers not to use their firearms but more importantly, at the time of the murder, Nichols had no knowledge or control over the troopers.[61]

On 27 March 1885, the Commissioner of Police referred Nichols' application for reinstatement in the Police Service to Colonial Secretary. His recommendation was that the application be denied:

> ... as regards his not being allowed sufficient latitude at the preliminary investigation held by Mr Inspector Isley in the Irvinebank murder case, I wired Mr Isley on the 3rd February to make a full inquiry and report; and again, on the 11th February hurried him to investigate "fully" and report and if Mr Nichols explanation was not satisfactory to suspend. In accordance with those instructions Mr Isley held an inquiry and not considering Mr Nichols explanation satisfactory suspended him. I feel certain that every latitude was given to Mr Nichols and his explanation which I forwarded on the 21 February was certainly not a satisfactory one.

---

61 For those who want to haggle over the point; see the trial and conviction of General Tomoyuki Yamashita, 1945.

> The troopers sent out scouting, looking for tracks should not have taken their arms. There is no excuse whatever for Mr Nichols' conduct in having discharged without taking them before a magistrate, as he says he did, two ~~aborigine~~ prisoners whom he had arrested on warrant. These prisoners have never been seen since.
>
> Mr Nichols had the character of being a willing hard-working officer during his nine years' service and no complaints of misconduct or harsh treatment of blacks has ever been made against him but I can see no cause for his conduct on the occasion under consideration and would ~~be sorry to~~ regret his being re-appointed to the police force.[62]

In the Police Gazette of 30 July 1892, the following appeared:

> Roma. 25 July 1892, W. A. Nicholl, alias Nichols, is charged, on warrant issued by the Roma Bench, with obtaining goods and money, to the value of £3 17s. 6d., from Louis Eugene Johnson, Club Hotel, on the 10th instant, by means of false verbal representations. Offender is an Englishman, about 42 years of age, 6 feet high, medium build, dark complexion, dark hair and beard (turning grey), about 12 stone weight, dark-brown eyes; wore light check tweed coat and vest, moleskin trousers, blucher boots, old soft felt hat with brim turned up. Says he is a drover, and that he has served in the Telegraph Department and Police Force. Was seen going towards Surat on foot. 24 October 1892, W. A. Nicoll, alias Nichols, charged with false pretences, has been arrested by the Tambo Police. He was remanded to Roma, where he was discharged by the Bench.[63]

As far as the record goes, Nichols' last official act was to apply for the Commonwealth old-age pension on 16 February 1921 at Adavale, Queensland, giving his particulars as William Austin Nichols arriving at the port of Brisbane by ship, Sir William Wallace, from St Katherine Docks,

---

62 QSA ID564169, folio 14, Nichols' Staff File.
63 Qld PG Vol. XXIX] 30 July 1892 [No. 31 p 274 & 360.

London in the latter part of 1875.⁶⁴

Regina v. Sambo, Sandy, Larry, Willie, Carlo, Jimmey & Pituri.

The committal proceedings were held at the Court House, Herberton before the police magistrate, W. M. Mowbray on 19 January 1885. The preliminary matters such as proof of arrest and the identification of the defendants was given in evidence by Barry. The charge read:

> On suspicion of having at Irvinebank, in the Police District of Herberton, on the eighteenth of October, A.D. 1884 conjointly feloniously and wilfully killed and murdered a male aboriginal known as "King Billy" of a female aboriginal known as "Kitty" of another female aboriginal name unknown and an aboriginal piccaninny name unknown.

When charged the troopers made no reply. This failure to reply was attributed by Barry to Sub-Inspector Carr's cautioning the troopers not to say anything after he had explained the charge to the troopers. Barry said he was astonished at Carr's illegal caution. Isley wrote to the Commissioner about the incident on 31 January 1885:

> With reference Det Barry's evidence in the troopers' case and concerning which I wired you urgent on 19th. When Sub-Inspector Carr at Barry's request explained the charge to the boys. Mr Carr said, "Say nothing." Barry objected. Mr Carr appealed to me. I told him to the effect that considering the boys ignorance of legal proceedings, I considered he was doing right and to go on. Mr Carr then continued if you say anything, it will be put on paper and made signs with his fingers of writing with his fingers on the palm of his other hand. I considered it was only just that the boys should fully know their position.
>
> On being recalled and re-sworn on 19th instant Barry could not

---

64 QSA ID564169, Nichols' Staff File.

remember this. To me the inference is obvious especially coupled with the manner in which he treated me and my officers (myself especially) as adverse witnesses.

While thanking you for taking these prosecutions out of my hands, I trust that should other cases occur where a detective is required in my district some other officer may be sent up. J B Isley.

Seymour's response: I must disapprove of Sub-Inspector Carr's action. It is evident that he was not anxious to facilitate the rights of justice. An officer of police is not justified in enticing or offering an accused person into making a confession of his guilt nor it is part of his duty to try to prevent him from making them. Inspector Isley's attitude in the matter is also unsatisfactory.[65]

John Bacey Isley stated five troopers were from Nigger Creek and two from Barron River (Willie and Jimmey). Irvinebank was within the Nigger Creek patrol area. Sub-Inspector Nichols did not send in any return showing he had patrolled the Irvinebank area. Troopers going on duty (patrol) were armed with a Snider rifle and cartridges. I cannot say whether they carried handcuffs, which were not part of their kit.

John Stewart, camp sergeant at Nigger Creek, deposed. My duty was to hand to troopers their Snider rifles, cartridges and handcuffs when going on patrol. I issued one pair each; I kept no record of numbers on the handcuffs. They returned on 19 October and returned the handcuffs.

Roland Walter Garraway deposed. On the fifteenth of October last (1884), I was stationed at Barron River Camp. I went to the Nigger Creek on the sixteenth of October last. My duty on that occasion was to get a deserter from Barron River camp, named Charlie. When we arrived at

---

65 QSA ID847148, 85/989.

Irvinebank the troopers pitched the tents. Next morning, the eighteenth, Sub-Inspector Nichols told me to send out Willie and Jimmey with the other troopers. They had each a Snider rifle and cartridge belt with cartridges. I cannot say whether they had handcuffs or not. They all started from the camp about ten o'clock in the morning and returned between nine and ten o'clock at night. The horses were brought back before the accused returned. Horses brought back by Charlie at sundown. Alicky came to the camp with a gin, spoke to Sandy and Nichols. Cartridges correspond, same red band. Flattened bullet same weight as bullet from snider cartridge. When boys returned, Sambo said "We can't catch Tommy think he gone away."

John Dwyer miner resided ten miles from Irvinebank, deposed. I saw troopers and Nichols arrest Spoopendyke. Friday before, killing a beast, gins about, troopers came and took two gins away. Did not know that one gin taken was called Kitty.

Alessandro Leoni woodcutter, deposed. My hut was half a mile from bodies. Heard five shots about an hour to hour and a half after dark and some crying near my camp; several more shots a good bit after that; next day went to look. Monday went to place of murder with mate, saw 4 bodies partially burnt no fire. Old man, two gins and piccaninny Went back with Moroney on Tuesday bodies same condition.

John Charles Sedgewick miner, deposed. On 18 October at my camp, about 7 or 7.30 pm, I heard 7 shoots; had to be by several persons. Shots came from direction of murder site. I saw black troopers about Irvinebank on 18 October.

George William Seaman deposed: I am a clerk in the employ of John Moffat and Co, and work at Irvinebank. On Friday, 17 October, I saw Nichols and some troopers at Irvinebank. There was another officer, Cadet Garraway. On Friday the troopers were scurrying about, I could not recognise any of them. On Saturday 18 October, I saw Nichols and Garraway at Irvinebank. There were some troopers there. After being marshalled, they left the camp on horseback. I did not see the troopers about at nightfall. I saw a trooper bringing home five or six horses up the road towards the camp.

The Police Magistrate: I don't know the trooper who brought the horses in.

Detective Barry: I was in the store on Saturday night at Irvinebank.

G. W. Seaman continued: On Sunday morning, 19 October, Alecky told me something. In consequence, I, John Moffat, Peter Moffat, Anthony Linedale, Charles Dineen and Evenden at about 9 o'clock started to go up a mountain near Irvinebank. Alicky took us to a blacks' camp. I saw the bodies of four blacks there; they were partially burned. One of the bodies was that of an old man named King Billy, the other was an old female known as Kitty, the third a female aboriginal, but was too much burnt to be recognisable. I saw Kitty alive between three and four on 18 October. The bodies were pretty well in a heap. They appeared to have been thrown together; there was no firewood about; some pieces of stick were not out. The bodies were still burning. I noticed that several saplings in this vicinity were marked as if the bark had been knocked off by bullets. Exhibit E appeared to be a flattened bullet. I produced it before the Court yesterday. I took it from one of the trees at a small distance away from the dead bodies. I got it on the Sunday morning. I also found the empty cartridge case within three or four feet of the bodies. On Wednesday, 14 January 1885, I visited the spot where the dead bodies were found with Detective Barry, and Constable Moroney. On that day Detective Barry and myself picked up the two empty cartridge cases marked exhibit C. The cartridge case found by me on Sunday 19 October and the two cartridge cases picked up by Detective Barry and myself on 14 January correspond in having a red band around them. I look at exhibit D (two empty cartridge cases) and compared them with the three other cartridge cases marked C. The two exhibits correspond as to the red band. In going, up the mountain Mr. Linedale, in my presence, picked up a pair of handcuffs. They were about two hundred yards from the dead bodies. I afterwards picked up a second pair myself. They were lying about 6 or 7 feet from the bodies. The two pairs of handcuffs produced (exhibit H) are those picked up by Linedale and myself. They bear the same numbers. I took possession of them until after the inquiry. On Wednesday 22 October, I again went back to the place where the bodies were in company with Constable Moroney and Leoni. The bodies were in the same position. The fire was not burning on that occasion, it was completely out. On Thursday, 23 October I again went to the scene in company with the Police Magistrate, Sergeant Breene, Constable Moroney, Dr. Bowkett, and Mr John Moffat; there was a fire burning on that occasion. Where the bodies were previously, no traces could be found.

To the Police Magistrate: In my opinion the bodies had been dead about 10 or 12 hours when seen on Sunday, 19 October. They could not have been dead longer as I recognised one of them whom I had seen alive the previous evening. The head of one of the gins appeared to have been smashed in.

To Detective Barry: I saw four bodies on Sunday morning, the fourth body was that of a piccaninny. I cannot say whether it was a male or female. Detective Barry and myself picked up the two cartridges just produced within a few feet of the heap of ashes where the dead bodies had previously been.

To the Police Magistrate: I do not remember seeing Alicky on Saturday 18th. I do not remember seeing him at Nichols' camp.

John Moffat deposed: I am a Magistrate of the Territory living at Irvinebank. I was at Irvinebank on 18 October last. I know Mr Seaman. I also know the boy Alicky. The blackboy Alicky took me and others to a mountain in the vicinity of Irvinebank. The others were George Seaman, Anthony Linedale, Peter Moffat, Charles Dineen and Evenden. On the way up the mountain I saw Anthony Linedale pick up pair of handcuffs about 200 yards from the dead bodies. I did not see any more handcuffs picked up, but afterwards saw a pair in George Seaman's possession which I was informed he had picked up. I saw the numbers on the handcuffs found. The numbers were 65 on one side and 79 on the other. One pair had a key with the number 39 on. The other pair had no key. I now look at exhibit H (two pairs handcuffs). I cannot say they are the same. I presume so as the numbers are the same. I did not see anything else picked up. Near where the second pair of handcuffs were picked up, I saw the bodies of four aboriginals. The bodies were dead and partially burned. I cursorily examined the bodies. One was the body of an old blackfellow, two others adult females and one was the body of a piccaninny whose sex did not appear. The bodies were laying side by side. Two with their heads one way and the other two in the other direction, the fire being in the middle of them. I had seen the body when alive which Alicky called King Billy. Alicky was the principal one who spoke and said it was King Billy. I did not observe any marks of violence on the bodies other than that caused by fire. The faces were lying somewhat downward and I could not tell whether they were disfigured. In consequence of what I saw, Mr. John Newell and me sent a telegram to the Police Magistrate who was in Thornborough. Mr Mowbray came out to Irvinebank on the Thursday following and I accompanied him, Dr. Bowkett, Mr Seaman, Sergeant Breene, and Constable Moroney to the spot where I had last seen the bodies. The place where the bodies previously were was occupied by the remains of a large fire. The fire was still smouldering; no bodies were then to be seen. I saw the fire raked by Constable Moroney. There were several pieces of bone brought out of the fire. One of them appeared to be a portion of a skull, but all of them were somewhat too charred for identification. I do not know Sub-Inspector Nichols. I saw black troopers about Irvinebank on Saturday 18 October. I think there were about half a dozen. I did not see any of them sufficiently near to be able to recognise them.

To the Police Magistrate: I believe Mr Seaman handed the handcuffs to Sergeant Breene in the presence of Moroney and the Police Magistrate.

When I first saw the bodies, from their appearance I thought they had been dead for more than 12 or 15 hours. That was between 9 and 10 o'clock on Sunday morning, 19 October last.

Denis Moroney deposed: I am a Constable of Police residing at Herberton. I was sent to Irvinebank on Wednesday, 22 October. I went to the top of a mountain at that place in company with George Seaman and Alessandro Leoni. I saw the bodies of four human beings. They were blacks; there were about four. There was an old fire where the bodies were. I will not swear the fire was out altogether. It was not burning brightly. I went again with the Police Magistrate and others on 23rd; I saw nothing but ashes on that occasion. I produced two pairs of handcuffs yesterday. I received them from Mr Moffat. The handcuffs produced bear the same numbers as the ones I received front Mr Moffat. It was after the inquiry into the death of the aboriginals that they were handed to me. I could not say whether the aboriginals I saw were male or female.

Alicky an aboriginal was called three times but did not appear. This closed the case for the Crown. The Police Magistrate said: It ought to be proved what place the prisoners were native of. Det Barry stated: That it was the custom in such cases to ask if the prisoners required assistance towards getting witnesses or whether they wanted an interpreter, if they did the Government would obtain one.

The Police Magistrate said there was no doubt in his mind that the blacks had been killed at Irvinebank; the evidence was not clear but there was a strong or probable presumption that either all the troopers or some of them were guilty. Where there was a strong or probable presumption of guilt he must commit for trial and leave it to the Attorney-General to enter a bill against them. When being asked if they had anything to say, all the prisoners replied no except Sambo who appeared to be in considerable perturbation of mind and twice commenced a statement but failed to get through.⁶⁶

The prisoners were committed for trial to the Supreme Court, Townsville for the sittings commencing 22 April 1885.

On 3 February 1885, Isley sent the following wire to the Commissioner of Police:

> Re Irvinebank, the seven troopers committed for trial left for Townsville Saturday, 31 January 1885; in event of no bill being filed will you please advise me at once that I may arrange to get the boys back again. They are too smart troopers for the police to lose if they should be discharged from custody.
>
> Seymour's response: These men will under no circumstances be employed in the NP force. I have already directed their dismissal and am surprised at this suggestion being put before me. 20.2.85.⁶⁷

The *Townsville Bulletin* of 25 April 1885 reported as follows:

> The case against the black troopers for the murder of certain aboriginals at Irvinebank, near Herberton, which has excited a great deal of interest throughout the North, did not come to a conclusion yesterday. At the outset, the difficulty of making the prisoners understand the terms of the information presented itself, and eventually proved to be insuperable. The interpreter of the court, after conferring with the prisoners, announced that he could not understand their language, and His Honour refused to allow the case to be conducted in "pigeon" English. The prisoners were, therefore, remanded until the next sittings of the court, it being suggested that in the meantime the prisoners might be instructed in English.⁶⁸

The proceedings of the trial of the five native troopers before his Honour

---

66   QSA ID 847145. *Herberton Advertiser* 24 January 1885 Vol. 5 No. 7.
67   QSA ID847145.
68   *Capricornian* 2 May 1885 p 8.

Mr. Justice Cooper at Townsville on 22 October 1885 for the Irvinebank murders were thus reported in the *Townsville Standard*:

> Willie, Sambo, Larry, Carlo, and Pituri, native troopers, were charged with the murder, of certain aboriginals at Irvinebank, in October last—namely, a male aboriginal named King Billy, a female aboriginal named Kitty, a female aboriginal name unknown. Mr. Virgil Power prosecuted for the Crown, and Mr. Ringrose appeared for the prisoners. On opening the case the Crown Prosecutor introduced a lad named William Buchanan, who had been brought from the Herbert River for the purpose of interpreting for one of the prisoners—Pituri—a Herbert River boy. His Honour carefully examined the lad as to his acquaintance with the native dialect, and elicited that he was 13 years of age, and acquired his knowledge of the language from hearing and speaking to the aboriginals employed on his father's farm. He told Pituri the offence with which he was charged, and received a rejoinder which appeared to be one of assent. His Honour then pointed out that if, after the boy had been sworn as an interpreter, in answer to such a charge as "Mr. Power says you killed other blacks" the prisoner replied "Yes", it might be construed into an admission of guilt. He asked Mr. Power if he considered the words were a charge of murder. Mr. Power replied "Yes." His Honour then said: "I strongly decline to send a man to the gallows on such an admission." The boy was then sworn, and communicated with the prisoners fluently, apparently making himself understood, but appeared to be unable to grasp the charges given him by his Honour, and shortly afterwards feeling unwell, he was allowed to leave the court.
>
> Paddy, an aboriginal, was next introduced to interpret for Carlo, but was not particularly successful, persisting in putting the charge as a question, and eliciting answers which, had they been received by the court, would have speedily decided the case. Another aboriginal, named Johnny, who appeared to interpret for Larry, Sambo, and Willie, was found to be quite unable to communicate the charge

to the prisoners, or even to grasp it himself, and on the Crown Prosecutor stating that no better interpreter could be obtained for the three prisoners mentioned above, his Honour discharged them, stating at the same time that he was not responsible for the case not proceeding. It was owing to the unsatisfactory state of the colony, and was a difficulty, that could not be overcome. He was there to administer the English law, and to see that the prisoners were tried according to that law, one of the first principles of which was that the prisoner should perfectly understand what was said and done in connection with the trial.

Paddy, who interpreted for Carlo, again endeavoured to make Carlo understand the nature of the charge preferred against him, but was not successful. In reply to his Honour, Inspector Morisset stated that he was convinced that Paddy, though a fairly intelligent boy, could not make Carlo understand either the charge or the evidence to be adduced. His Honour then said if Inspector Morisset was certain that Paddy could not make Carlo understand he did not see how he could be sufficiently certain that Paddy could interpret properly, and he would therefore discharge Carlo.

A black boy named Tommy was then called in to assist Buchanan to interpret for the only remaining prisoner Pituri, and the trial proceeded. After another attempt to communicate with the prisoner by both interpreters—both of whom appeared to disagree—his Honour asked Inspector Morisset to state his opinion with reference to the reliability and intelligence of the lad Buchanan. Inspector Morisset replied that the lad had only gone to school within the last eight months, and was evidently ignorant of a number of common English words. For instance, he believed Buchanan did not understand the meaning of the word "charge." After a short conversation with the boy Buchanan, the Crown Prosecutor said that he had asked him the meaning of the word "charge," and he had replied that it meant to "bill" a person with an account. This definition of the word decided his Honour in not accepting Buchanan's services, and as the Crown Prosecutor stated he had not a better qualified one to bring forward the prisoner was discharged.

His Honour said that he was convinced that if the case had proceeded slips might have happened which would have caused injustice to be done which they would never have been able to repair. The prisoners appeared to be exceedingly relieved at being discharged, although, with the exception of Larry, they were all in capital health. Larry, however, was much thinner than he was on his last appearance in court. Although not understanding English sufficiently to hold intelligent converse, the prisoners perfectly understood the order to leave the dock, the first three discharged leaving the box without hesitation, while the two remaining made an attempt to follow.[69]

Alicky, the blackfellow, whose absence at the prosecution of the Native Trooper re Irvinebank atrocities at the Herberton Police Court, was brought into Herberton by Sergeant Breene on 16 April 1885, but very shortly afterwards jumped the Barracks fence and made for the hills, with the Sergeant and a couple of Constables in hot pursuit. After attaining the summit of a steep hill Alicky's boots became his bane. In vain he endeavoured to get rid of them before his pursuers approached, and, finding himself unable to accomplish this, he set to work pelting the Constables with stones — two of whom he hit violently — until utterly exhausted — he was easily recaptured. In the charge of Sergeant Breene, Alicky left Herberton on 17 April en route for Townsville.[70]

The Commissioner of Police received information from Inspector Isley, Port Douglas, under date 28 September 1885, that Constable John Stewart, of the Mosman Native Mounted Police, had been seriously injured by a kick from a horse on 27 September. A subsequent telegram stated that

---

69 *Western Star* and *Roma Advertiser* 11 November 1885 p 3. The charge against Sandy and Charlie was dropped.
70 *Capricornian* 2 May 1885 p 8. *Herberton Advertiser* 18 April 1885.

Constable Stewart died on 4 October 1885.[71]

On 23 February 1996, the Eacham Historical Society members and others conducted a field trip to locate and dig the murder site of the four Aborigines at Irvinebank. The site was said to be located "on top of a ridge between Graveyard and Fireclay Gullies, at 900 metres elevation." Although the team had GPS, they have not seen fit to publish the coordinates of the site. The dig of the site produced many finds. Perhaps the most interesting were the location of 8 Snider cartridge cases and 8 pieces of lead projectiles. These items when put together with the 3 Snider cartridge cases and the flattened projectile placed in evidence at the committal proceedings, certainly confirm the evidence of John Charles Sedgewick, miner who heard on 18 October 1884 at his camp, about 7 or 7.30 pm, 7 shots.[72]

---

71 *Queenslander* 10 October 1885 p 573. Reg No. 317 Const John Stewart died 5 October 1885, Qld PG Vol. XXII] 24 October 1885 [No. 22 p 259.
72 *Failure of Justice: the story of the Irvinebank Massacre* / written by Geof Genever; additional information written by Duncan Ray, Tony Derksen [and] Henry Tranter, Malanda, Qld.: Eacham Historical Society, Reprint Second Edition, May 2010 pp 18-19.

5

Public Comment

I have included this chapter because I feel it is essential that the reader of today has an opportunity to peruse what the community of yesteryear read in their newspapers each day as the Irvinebank incident unfolded before them. Some historians make an effort to canvass the historical press coverage of an incident under study. Many do not and those who do, merely provide a cursory review of the material, giving little weight to the content. The Black Armband school of thought when they deign to look at this material, take a haughty stance and cherry pick the material to suit their own agenda. This is because they see the historical press as a useless European source containing all the well-known prejudices of the past such as: discrimination, class exploitation, racism and colonial dispossession just to name a few. The style of presentation of the material I have adopted in this chapter may not suit every reader but I am of the view that the robust approach of cut and paste format is more appropriate in a monograph such as this.

In the following material reference is made to the Hopeful cases where Neil McNeil and Bernard Williams were convicted of murdering natives while their vessel was recruiting labour at the D'Entrecasteaux group. Widespread and earnest agitation was started for a reprieve of the death sentences. This was partly based on a doubt whether the evidence fully established the death of the victims, and therefore whether the offence technically amounted to murder.[73]

A meeting of the Cairns Progress Association was held on Tuesday, 27 May 1884, present: Messrs. R. J. Gordon (in the chair), S. Cochrane, S. L. S. Rodds, J. MacNamara, L. Severin, D. Patience, and F. T. Wimble.

Proposed by Mr. Fred. T. Wimble, seconded by Mr. Severin, and carried, "That application be made to the Commissioner of Police to have the native police camp now under Sub-Inspector Carr, and stationed on the Upper Barron, removed to the reserve at the head of the inlet, Trinity Bay; there being a reserve there which would be central for the purpose, while the present situation of the camp is found to be totally in adequate for the requirements of the district. If the application be granted it would provide safety to the numerous settlers on the Russell, Mulgrave and Freshwater rivers, and Smithfield, all of which districts are suffering from the depredations of the blacks.

Letter to the Editor of the *Cairns Post* of 7 August 1884:

> Seeing by your journal that an agitation is on foot in Cairns for the removal of Sub-Inspector Carr and his troopers to the Mulgrave River, in order to afford better protection to the settlers there against the blacks, I should like to give my experience of Mr. Carr

---

73   *Brisbane Courier* 31 December 1884 p 3.

and the construction he places upon the duties of himself and the native police he commands. Being a settler in the district over which Inspector Carr holds sway, and suffering great losses from the blacks, I applied to him for protection, but only received in reply an intimation that he and his troopers were stationed in the district to protect the blacks, not to punish them. I am not aware if this is really the case, but if it is, I fail to see what use he is to the white population here, or would be to the Mulgrave settlers if transferred to their vicinity. But I have reason to believe that Inspector Carr studies his own pleasure rather than his duties, whatever they may be, and in substantiation of this opinion I can mention several recent dates when he has been absent for days together on simply pleasure excursions, and taken his troopers with him. I give three of these occasions.

On the 21st June he attended the Masonic Ball at Herberton, and was absent three to four days, taking with him his 2nd officer, 6 troopers, and 12 horses. I may here mention that Herberton is not in his district. Two or three days after his return, he went to Port Douglas, and attended the Bachelor's Ball, being absent 2 days, and again taking 6 troopers and 12 horses. On the 10th July he proceeded to the Western, again visiting Herberton. My object in bringing this matter before the public is to show that a large sum of money is annually expended to keep up an establishment which is no protection or service to anyone. I speak feelingly on this subject, as my own losses from the depredations of the blacks have not been less than £1 per day for the past seven years, and latterly matters have been worse than ever. Trusting the publication of this letter will attract attention to the subject. John Atherton, Emerald End, August 2nd, 1884.[74]

Letter to Editor of *Cairns Post*, 28 August 1884:

Sir, I notice in different issues of your paper that the officer in charge

---

74   *Cairns Post* 7 August 1884 p 2.

of native police here is accused of negligence in the performance of his duty. I think there must be some mistake in making this assertion, as I can confidently state there is not a more hard-worked officer in the service than Sub-Inspector Nichols, nor one that has given more protection to the settlers. No doubt as Cairns is becoming an important place it needs more protection, but this, I would suggest, should be derived from a separate detachment, provided specially for that district. Yours, &c., AMICUS Herberton, August 28, 1884. [The correspondence referred to by "Amicus" did not mention or apply to Sub-Inspector Nichols. Ed. C. P.][75]

The following tale of horrors appeared in the *Northern Standard* of 3 November 1884:

It appears that on the 14th of October Sub-Inspector Nichols applied to Mr. Hewell, J.P., (sic, Newell) for two warrants for the arrest of two blackboys supposed to be connected with the late Walsh murder. On obtaining the same he and his black troopers set out for Irvinebank and arrested two natives there named Spoopendyke and Toby, although they were informed that the blacks arrested had never been out of the camp and did not at all resemble the description given of the two boys for whose arrest the warrants had been issued. Spoopendyke, who had fought like a fiend when arrested, presented a terrible sight when overcome and tied to a fence, and kept frantically howling in his own language for spears and other weapons. Toby, who was of a different disposition, made no resistance at all. The latter black had been in the employ of Mr. Moffat, and that gentleman assured him that no harm would come of the arrest as he was innocent of the charge. Toby however was not to be comforted. The prisoners were led out of the camp, and as they have never been seen since, it is surmised that they have been destroyed, regardless of the fact that, as they were in the hands of the law, having been arrested on warrant, the law should have been

---

75 *Cairns Post* 28 August 1884 p 3. See *Cairns Post* 3 July 1884 p 3, Re Sub-Inspector Carr.

permitted to take its course. Had the white residents of the camp known that such an end was intended, the troopers would never have been allowed to remove them. I forgot to mention that in the struggle Spoopendyke got the thumb of the sub-inspector's orderly between his teeth and held on until the handcuffs had been freely used on his head. The sub-inspector afterwards patted him on the head and was rewarded for so doing at once, the prisoner spitting straight in his face. This action of Spoopendyke doubtless precipitated their fate, if it did not decide it. Unsatisfied with this little escapade, the orderly and seven black troopers returned on Sunday, the 19th, to Irvinebank, and as soon as the blacks saw them coming, they took to the hills. At this time the residents of Irvinebank were unaware that Spoopendyke and Toby had been removed from this 'vale of tears.' All the next day the troopers scoured the ranges in pursuit, with what result is not known. They, however, overlooked one camp which they suspected was close handy, but could not drop upon, and which contained a decrepit old man named 'King Billy.' A blackboy named Alecky, who is employed at a public house, told the orderly that 'he knew where King Billy sit down,' and on being promised 'two fellow tomahawk' and 'two fellow blanket' if he would lead the troopers to the place, he consented and indicated a high spur about a mile and a half from the town as the place of refuge. An Italian charcoal burner, who resides at the foot of the spur, noticed the troopers stealthily ascending it and shortly afterwards heard shots and screams. According to Alecky's version, King Billy was shot while asleep. Tommy, a black about 20 years of age, who was the only other male in the camp, jumped over a precipice and escaped—which is little short of marvellous, as the rock from which he leaped was covered with bullet marks. Two gins and a piccaninny still remained in the camp, the elder of them—King Billy's spouse—took hold of a 'waddy' and began to abuse the troopers, when one of them clubbed his rifle and beat her brains in. The other gin was then shot in company with the piccaninny, which was about 6 years old. A fire was then made, and the bodies thrown into it.

THE IRVINEBANK MASSACRE

The troopers then returned to Irvinebank, and, in company with the orderly (Stewart by name), left for Herberton the next morning at daylight. Alecky, however, soon began to relate the previous night's doings, and on his assertions coming to the ears of Mr. Moffat who is a justice of the peace, that gentleman determined to inquire into the matter, and ordered Alecky to conduct him to the spot. This was done, and the bodies of the blacks were identified as the remains of King Billy and two well-known gins. The piccaninny, however, could not be identified. By a strange chance, the faces of all the victims remained uninjured. Mr. Moffat immediately rode into town to acquaint Mr. Mowbray, police magistrate, with the circumstances, but that gentleman was absent in Thornborough. A policeman was sent out to view the bodies, and by whom it was ascertained that Mr. Mowbray would hold an inquiry on the Thursday. On that day Mr. Mowbray left town with Dr. Bowkett for Irvinebank to inquire into the matter, but on arriving there and visiting the scene of the slaughter, not a vestige of human remains were visible, a large fire having been evidently built on them the previous night.

Notwithstanding this unexpected turn, evidence was taken, and the facts clearly proved, there being over fifty persons who had seen the bodies. A number of cartridges with the Government stamp and a couple of pairs of handcuffs were found the morning after the occurrence. The evidence has been forwarded to the Colonial Secretary, and it is probable further inquiry will be made.[76]

The following is commentary from the Herberton correspondent of the Brisbane *Telegraph*:

Last week I alluded to the discovery of seven dead Aboriginals half consumed by fire, alleged to have been 'dispersed.' Since then, at a few miles from the same place two prospectors came across a blacks' camp in which they found a miscellaneous lot of stolen articles, including axes, tomahawks, rope, a woman's dress, &c., &c., showing

---

76 Reproduced in the *Brisbane Courier* 14 November 1884 p 5.

the continuous depredations being perpetrated by the niggers. The necessity of some check against the blacks is very apparent, and however it may shock people, the episode near Irvinebank is the result of the system which precludes the possibility of discrimination. It is believed that the legalised 'dispersion' causes retaliation; my experience of the niggers is quite the reverse; theft is their predominant mania, and when they take life it is with a view to robbery. The matter of the blacks is one that the north cannot argue with the south; simply because the latter are not within reach of the wild niggers and they can conceive nothing that they are capable of doing. 'Dispersing' the thieving niggers in the north is considered very cruel, but despatching a man-of-war to burn down villages, and kill the populations with shells, is considered comme il faut by the more civilised people of the south. What is required in these scrubby parts are native troopers under a modified system, so that whatever is done be above board. If 'dispersion,' as understood well everywhere, be necessary, let the Government who orders it be responsible, but not, as now, issue certain instructions to officers, who are supposed to carry them out, but who, if unfortunately found out, become the victims. This is unfair and unjust. There must be a special police protection against the darkies, or invasion and wholesale murder will ensue; how to organise that protection is the difficulty, without such events as the one near Irvinebank occurring. That the innocent often suffers for the guilty is true enough, but the recent murder of Morgan and Bailey has given work to troopers, who are not prone to be discriminating when on the warpath.[77]

The *Maryborough Chronicle, Wide Bay and Burnett Advertiser* provided the following out of court statement of John Moffat, mill owner, Irvinebank, justice of the peace:

> ... the blacks whose bodies were identified were quite inoffensive creatures; he also stated that the blackboy who led them to the place

---

77 Telegraph 10 November 1884 p 2.

informed him that the blacks killed were asleep when he and the troopers arrived at the mountain top; that the troopers surrounded the camp and fired on them; that one of them started up and ran down the other side of the mountain, and that he himself ran home to Irvinebank; on the side of the mountain towards which the black boy indicated the blackfellow had run, and about fifty yards from the camp, the bullet was taken out of a tree; near it were found a spear and woomera, on the latter of which were traces of blood; the party who went out to search for the remains left the blackboy in the vicinity, looking for the missing man, and when they returned to Irvinebank they found three troopers had been inquiring for the blackboy, whom they wanted to take.[78]

Letter to the Editor of the *Brisbane Courier* by A. Meston.

SIR, Another commission is urgently wanted to inquire into the native police system. It will be found, I believe, that most of the expenditure in that direction is an entirely unwarranted waste of public money. At the present time there are about 200 black troopers and trackers, whose wages amount to £1600 and rations to £7000. If we add to this the salaries of the officers, horses, accoutrements, clothes, rifles, cartridges, and other contingencies and incidentals, we shall find that our black police cost Queensland about £15,000 or £20,000 per annum. That most of the money is foolishly thrown away can be clearly shown by investigation. It is also well for the colony to know what system the black police pursue towards the natives. Probably there will be some startling disclosures made, provided the witnesses are allowed to restrict themselves to facts only and no names revealed.

Northern men who have seen raids by the troopers or by white men are not likely to mention names, though they may readily disclose the circumstances. It will be enough if the commission discover enough to warrant the abolition of the black police. The pioneer

---

78 *Maryborough Chronicle, Wide Bay and Burnett Advertiser* 25 December 1884 p 2.

settlers can take care of themselves, and if they have occasionally to shoot blacks from necessity, they will not shoot them for sport nor slaughter gins and piccaninnies. The Irvinebank affair is not exceptional, except in being discovered. I am quite satisfied that Sub-inspector Nichols had nothing to do with it. He is one of the most efficient and faithful officers in the whole police force. Every officer of native police knows that his troopers, under certain circumstances, will go off on little excursions of their own and slaughter all ages and sexes indiscriminately. The officer may only hear accidentally long afterwards what was done during the expedition.

I know of one case among several others where an officer and his trooper shot seventeen blacks in one spot, and the troopers disappeared for two days and returned with a little boy about eight years of age, the sole survivor of a whole camp. And all this was to avenge the death of a kanaka! Of course, the officer could not be held justly responsible for the camp extermination any more than Nichols for the Irvinebank business. The difference lies between the known and the unknown. One officer has since been promoted, and Nichols has been dismissed. [It] is a thankless and unpleasant position. If a native police officer is to be any use at all he must occasionally shoot blacks, if he never shoots them, he is neither use nor ornament. However humane an officer maybe he cannot always control his troopers. Every northern man knows how preposterous is the idea that the officer can always keep his men in sight among the tropical scrubs of the north. Undoubtedly it is necessary sometimes to shoot blacks. The rifle is the only argument they can understand, but the Government incur a serious responsibility in turning loose a couple of hundred black bloodhounds, cruel as tigers, to massacre whole camps for offences for which a white man might get only a short term of imprisonment. I allude to killing cattle and stealing from settlers. We have less consideration for our own blacks than for the South Sea cannibals. Every month in North Queensland there are cases of kidnapping worse than those of the Hopeful, and most of the black police in the service of the Queensland Government are guilty of acts which make those of McNeil and Williams appear to be harmless pastime. It is historical folly at this hour of the day to rush round looking for sacrifices to vengeance. It is worse folly to attempt to tinker with either the system of black police or the labour traffic. Better to candidly admit the scandalous abuses inevitably attendant on both systems, and sweep them away for ever.[79]

The *Queensland Figaro* descended into a journalistic outpouring of melodramatic drivel and sheer hyperbolic madness:

> I herewith solemnly impeach Samuel Walker Griffith, Premier of Queensland, with being the aider and abettor of murders so foul that a hideous hell is let in upon the land when they are contemplated. I impeach him with having winked at the escape of a wealthy murderer, whose black heart was shown to have had no pity, and the recital of whose black deeds affright the imagination. I empanel the public of Queensland as my jury, and, in the name of justice, of humanity, and of everything that is not dastardly, cruel and murderous, do I demand of that public to judge between Mr. Griffith and me, his accuser.
>
> I am going to paint a contrast to the McNeil episode. Every reader knows how all the machinery and money at the command of the Government were brought into requisition against Neil McNeil, who now stands condemned to be hanged, for an alleged murder in the South Seas; but who, I contend, is to be hanged as the victim of a fad by which the present Government seeks to hypocritically whitewash itself in the eyes of blind admirers. I am going to show, you that a crime a hundred times more hideous has just been perpetrated in our own colony of Queensland—perpetrated by a paid murderer of the Queensland Government; and that this horrible outrage has been winked at, and the murderer been permitted to escape, by the very same Government that wants to hang Neil McNeil.

---

79 *Brisbane Courier* 27 December 1884 p 3.

PUBLIC COMMENT

That worm of papers, the Brisbane *Telegraph*, the only Brisbane supporter of the present Government, expressed indignation the other day, because the *Courier*, the leading and a just journal, pointed out that Mr. Griffith, when Attorney-General in 1876, permitted to escape from justice Sub-Inspector Wheeler, who beat a black gin to death with strands of telegraph wire under the most horrible circumstances. Well, I will let that case slide. I will, for the sake of cutting the ground from under the feet of those who uphold Griffith in that act, ignore it, altogether as a forgotten horror, and assume that Sam Griffith, being then young in office, couldn't help himself. But I charge you all to read the thrilling atrocities I am now about to describe. Remember this is no fancied tale—no exaggerated fact—no invention. It appeared in the *Courier* of November 14th; it has been alluded to in Parliament, and even Sam Griffith himself has hinted that murder most foul has been committed; and it has been more or less fully ventilated in almost every paper in the Colony.

I think it fitting at the present moment, as the most Mephistophelian commentary upon the case of Neil McNeil, to give the full and true details of this revolting outrage. And its results. On October 14th, Sub-Inspector Nichols applied to Mr. Hewell, J.P., Herberton, for two warrants for the arrests of two blackfellows supposed to have been implicated in a recent murder on the Walsh River. Hewell issued the warrants. Sub-Inspector Nichols and his black troopers thereupon set out for Irvinebank. There, they arrested two blackfellows known as "Spoopendyke" and "Toby," although they were reliably informed that these boys had never been out of the camp, and although the boys did not, in any particular, resemble those described in the warrants.

"Spoopendyke" fought fiercely against arrest, but was overcome and tied down to a fence. "Toby" made no resistance whatever, but cried bitterly. This "Toby" had been in the employ of Mr. Moffat, J.P., and was a peaceable, useful fellow. Mr. Moffat advised him to go quietly, assuring him that he was now in the hands of the law, and that no harm could possibly come to him, British justice always protecting the innocent. Ah! if it only did! Those two prisoners were led out of camp under formal arrest, and have never been seen since!

They were the first two victims of the blood thirsty murderer, Sub-Inspector Nichols. Says the local correspondent:

Had the white residents of the camp known that such an end was intended, the troopers would never have been allowed to remove them. But the work of bloody murder had only commenced. The troopers returned to Irvinebank on Sunday, Oct. 19th. As soon as the blacks saw them, they took to the hills. All next day, these hell-hounds scoured the ranges, but the blacks had securely hidden themselves. Baulked of more victims, they sought out a black boy named "Alecky," who is working at a public house, and offered him "two fellow tomahawk and two fellow blanket," if he would guide them to where "old King Billy sit down." "Alecky" consented. "King Billy" was a decrepit old man who could hardly hurt a child; "Alecky" led the gore thirsting hand of Government murderers to "King Billy's" camp. An Italian charcoal-burner, who resides at the foot of the spur, on the top of which was "King Billy's" camp, saw the troopers stealthily crawling up the range and watched them. As soon as they reached the top, this charcoal-burner heard shots and screams.

From "Alecky's" evidence, the details of the outrage are these. The troopers shot crippled "King Billy" while the old man was asleep. "Tommy" a young black about 20 years of age, jumped over a precipice and escaped, the rock he leaped over being plentifully riddled with bullets. There were two gins and a piccaninny yet in the camp. The elder, who was "King Billy's" wife, lifted a waddy in her withered and weak arms and uttered some words of abuse. A trooper clubbed his rifle and bashed her skull in. The young gin and piccaninny were then shot. Ay, and what besides, as I shall ask presently? A fire was made and the bodies thrown into it. This made five innocent victims brutally murdered. The troopers returned quietly to Irvinebank and then went on to Herberton. But the cold-blooded fiends had forgotten to shoot "Alecky," their guide; and "Alecky," and the Italian charcoal-burner began to talk, and people began to listen. Moffat, who is a J.P., got "Alecky" to guide him to the locality, and the bodies of these poor murdered people were found half-burnt in the ashes of a smouldering fire. Over fifty persons saw the corpses. That of the piccaninny was unrecognisable. All the others were, however, clearly identified, as an avenging Nemesis had not permitted the fire to injure their faces. Fifty persons identified them as having been well-known and peaceable blacks, resident always in camp.

Mr. Moffat immediately rode into Herberton, to acquaint the P. M., Mowbray, with what he had seen and heard. Mr. Mowbray was unfortunately away at Thornborough, and could not get to the place before Thursday, October 23rd. Meanwhile, a Herberton constable had formally viewed the bodies. On the 23rd, Police Magistrate Mowbray and Dr. Bowkett proceeded to the scene of the murders, when, lo! not a vestige of the crime remained. A second large fire had evidently been built over the bodies, and that, too, only the previous night! In what bush recess lie the remains of "Spoopendyke" and "Toby," no one knows. Perhaps, these, too, were burnt.

Mowbray held what investigation he could. A number of cartridges, bearing the Government stamp, were found on the spot. Further, a couple of pairs of handcuffs were found in the ashes of the fire. To what hideous secret—to what horrible additional crimes were those handcuffs the key? Bushmen will not hesitate to think, even if they won't say, that the young gin and the piccaninny were handcuffed the while their murderers ravished them. Oh God! And these foul deeds happen under the Government of the "great and good Samuel." I want the reader to keep Neil McNeil, the condemned man, once more in a corner of his mind. Listen, and contrast the dealings with McNeil with how Government has dealt with this brutal fiend Nichols. Mowbray's report and the depositions he took were sent in, not to the Attorney-General, but to Samuel Walker Griffith, Premier of Queensland. What has resulted? The punishment dealt out for these atrocious murders may be read of as a calm, common-place piece of news in a paragraph contained in the *Courier* of December 10th, and which piece of unstartling news reads thus:

> As a result of the Magisterial enquiry held by Mr. Mowbray, the Government has dispensed with the services of Sub-Inspector W. Nichols, and the black troopers engaged in the raid have been discharged. "Dispensed with the services!" Ye Gods! My blood boils when I think of it. Can you, reader, wonder now when I state that the condemned man, Neil McNeil, is the victim of a political fad— the sacrifice that is to be offered on the altar of Sam Griffith's political advancement? You cannot. I may now add, from information received by me from reliable sources that the murderer Nichols has escaped from Queensland in a bêche-de-mer vessel. Will the crawling *Telegraph* excuse Sam's share in this miscarriage of justice? What cares Nichols for dismissal? He is wealthy. Ah! and McNeil is poor —very poor, and has a wife and family to support. Can anyone call this even-handed justice? I solemnly impeach Samuel Walker Griffith, Premier of Queensland, as having been guilty of the awful crime of shutting his eyes to the commission of a crime still more awful, and of thus being particeps criminis in it, by letting a hired Government assassin escape from justice.[80]

The *Telegraph* responded as follows:

> I note that a Brisbane paper was very severe on ex-Sub-Inspector Nichols re the raid on the blacks at Irvinebank, but the information anent Nichols was all wrong, as he had not left in a bêche-de-mer vessel, but is here laid up with fever, from which he is only now recovering. Further, he is by no means a rich man — the contrary — and a purse of sovereigns were presented to him by those who know how he stood financially. With regard to this matter, it is only just to say that the actual deed was generally condemned here, but as the circumstances are better known and better understood in

---

80 *Queensland Figaro* 13 December 1884 p 3.

the district than in Brisbane, the same degree of onus is not laid to Nichols, seeing that he was not present at the outrage, and people know the extremes to which black troopers will go when they commence to do battle with a strange tribe. Outside people, miners and settlers, without for a moment advocating similar cruelties, view, with more moderation the difficulties that present themselves to prevent the loss of life and property without the aid of the native police. They argue further, and rely, as it were, upon inspectors of native police assisting them against attacks by the blacks, and look upon such aid as their rights, seeing that they are taxed to pay the cost of the required supervision, and the cost of rifles and cartridges. Who can doubt what that aid really means?[81]

Editorial of the *Herberton Advertiser* of 28 January 1885:

The discharge from custody of Mr W. A. Nichols at the Police Court this week was generally considered a foregone conclusion by everyone who heard and read the evidence given in the case of the Crown versus seven Native Troopers charged with the murder of blacks at Irvinebank in October last. That the ex-Inspector should have been arrested and incarcerated at so early a period does not reflect credit upon the judgment of the Colonial Secretary who, as a lawyer, must have comprehended the many suspicious circumstances that may surround a man and yet that man be innocent of a charge preferred against him. What to a layman appears definite and complete evidence of guilt, to a lawyer—a Barrister particularly—has a very different aspect. In this case the arrest of Mr. Nichols upon the charge of being accessory before the fact could with more reason have been delayed until the hearing of the charge made against the seven troopers who now stand committed for trial for murder, as it was a well-known fact that he was on his way to headquarters to request that his explanation of the unhappy affair be made public and to publicly refute the statement made in a Brisbane sensational publication. That a murder, horrible in itself and alike horrible to the

---

81 *Telegraph* 3 January 1885 p 2.

community in whose precincts it was perpetrated, was committed, there can exist, no doubt, and those who were the means of bringing the murderers to justice cannot be too highly commended; but it must be borne in mind, however disagreeable it may be to recognise it, that this fatal deed and many similar ones have arisen out of a system albeit legalised by the distribution of guns and ammunition to blacks, which should never have been introduced into a British Colony or countenanced by successive colonial Governments. That the Native Trooper Corps have a deterrent effect has been proved in this district, but that its dismemberment without substitutes on a reformed system, will bring sorrow and grief to the community we regret to have to predict. Yet that the officer in charge, under the existing system, should be held amenable for the atrocities perpetrated in his absence by semi-civilised savages sent in pursuit to apprehend a deserter of the same colour but of a different tribe and consequently looked upon as a natural enemy, appears anomalous. The evidence adduced shows that the Blacks were instructed to bring in a deserter named "Tommy." Now, who can tell who were "Tommy's" friends and what cropped up to cause the unfortunate slaughter of the innocent blacks at Irvinebank. The latter may or may not have interfered between Tommy and the Troopers, or for causes undivulged the natural animosity between tribes may have incited those possessing firearms to shoot down those who had none, and what appears to the British mind an act of cowardice may have a contrary interpretation by aboriginal custom. If we thought Nichols culpable or capable of committing a cold-blooded murder, we would be amongst the first to condemn him, but we do not believe it; and although we are very strongly averse to the policy of the Griffith Government, we decline to help to make Nichols or anyone else a victim as a remonstrance against that policy.

Why did not Nichols accompany the Troopers? This is a question that may be replied to simply by stating that Mr Nichols, as an officer of ten years standing was thoroughly conversant with the unpublished regulations of the service and obeyed instructions. As adduced in evidence his presence where the capture of a deserter was desired was unnecessary and in despatching troopers for that purpose, he could not foresee what was likely to transpire between them and the blacks who lost their lives. Although, according to Inspector Isley's evidence Nichols' erred in judgment by sending out so large a scouting party. It was generally understood that Nichols took his boys out to apprehend two supposed murderers of Morgan and Bailey on a warrant signed by a local magistrate, but this magistrate was unaware of any other private mission being intrusted to the Inspector. The suspected blacks were arrested with a view to bring them to Herberton, but "Tommy" the deserter, it is alleged caused a general RENCONTRE and those who had the firearms were the conquerors.

Detective Barry conducted his case admirably well and manifested considerable legal acumen but he could not overcome the incontrovertible fact that Nichols was not present at what occurred and as well might Sub-Inspector Carr be held responsible for two of his detachment being in the affray. If the circumstances adduced in evidence will be the means of ventilating and introducing an efficient system of police protection of equal deterrent capacity much good will have been done and the principal movers in making the affair public will be honourably remembered by the colony. Nonetheless, Nichols has undergone a fiery ordeal from which he has emerged scatheless; he has been the victim of a legalised but barbarous system and of sensational Brisbane illustrations which latter have gone a long way to secure sympathy for him, because McNeil and Williams' case, in whose behalf they were introduced, required no further victims to ensure public sympathy. With regard to the cold-blooded catastrophe referred to, it has called forth a general sentiment of deprecation and a feeling of disgust that such a thing should be countenanced and paid for by a Christian Government. Police protection is urgently necessary but the public will be more satisfied if that protection be deterrent without invoking the aid of cowardly murders and conduce to the better conditions of the blacks of the country.[82]

The *Cairns Post* was most pessimistic about the Irvinebank murders and what they held for the future:

> There are two events, taken in connection one with the other, that give rise to serious thoughts—these are the murder of McAulay by the blacks on the Mulgrave River, and the arrest of ex-sub-inspector Nichols, charged on suspicion with being accessory to the murder of blacks at Irvinebank. The real murderers of McAulay will not be punished, simply because the real culprits will not be caught, and this foul murder will remain unavenged as was that at the Russell River. The sad affair at Irvinebank is likely to be avenged, but again the actual murderers will go "scot-free," and although the issue may be fruitless Nichols will be a great sufferer in mind. The real charge upon which the ex-Inspector will be arraigned—if the Attorney-General files a bill—will be for the crime of having been "bowled out," although other words in legal parlance will be substituted. The effect of this arrest will be most certainly a continual repetition of the sad McAulay murder, merely because no native police inspector however experienced and prudent he may be, will run the risk of being "turned" on, and the fate of Nichols will be the salvation of any number of murderous niggers. I am a dead enemy to cold-blooded murders be the victim white or black, but when blacks are pitted against their brethren with the one-sided advantage of having in their possession firearms furnished by the Government, it is hardly just to criminally punish the officer in charge for a breach of discipline by not being present at an affray, especially if that breach has been already punished by dismissal from the service. The real sufferers by the Irvinebank tragedy will be the public, settlers, and travellers, as the niggers will soon discover a change in the tactics of police officers, of which they will not fail to take every advantage. If Mr. Nichols' troubles will be the means of com-

---

82 Vol. V. No. 8.

pletely annihilating the black police system, and end at that, the
public will have much to thank him for, because a far better course
can be adopted to protect the white settlers and their property. The
blacks must be prevented from perpetrating outrages; this cannot
be affected by kindness, therefore other means must be made available, and the disciples of Exeter Hall should be able to submit some
measure to meet the case.[83]

The Brisbane *Telegraph*'s Herberton correspondent provided the following:

The committal of the troopers, which meant the breaking up of the
station here, as five of them formed the detachment, has caused
considerable alarm, and a largely attended meeting was held on
Wednesday evening to protest against leaving the district without
police protection, in the face of its being known that a detachment
of native troopers are under orders to make a long patrol at the Mulgrave and Russell rivers. The inevitable consequence of this will be
the blacks from there will come up this way, and there is reason
to fear that what occurred here before will be repeated. The result
of Nichols' case has given general satisfaction; firstly, because he
is considered a most efficient officer; secondly, because he is the
victim of a Brisbane sensational paper; and thirdly, because, having
undergone a most searching inquiry, he has been cleared of the imputations charged against him; which may be the means of changing
the whole system into something better and equally deterrent in its
character. Some plan may be formulated to improve the condition of
the blacks, which may tend to lessen evils on both sides; and I am of
opinion that the country would contribute towards such a scheme
with more pleasure than paying troopers, if it had the effect of stopping outrages. My correspondence has appeared weekly in your
columns close upon eight years, during which period I have written
largely and frequently upon the subject of blacks under different re-

---

83 *Cairns Post* 8 & 15 January 1885 p 2 & *Cairns Post* 29 January 1885 p 3. See pages 29 - 33 above.

gimes, till at last, I have arrived at the conclusion above expressed.[84]

The Irvinebank Tragedy, letter to The Editor.

Sir, I take the liberty of asking you to find room for this in the columns of your paper, as I know, considerable interest in the atrocious murder of aboriginals at Irvinebank has been manifested in some of the Brisbane papers. By some of the Press the Government has been twitted with allowing murderers at our own doors to go unpunished, while 'so much fuss has been made over the Hopeful case.' I have always been of the opinion that the present Government were perfectly sincere in their efforts to check the abuses of the black labour traffic in the South Seas, and when information reached here that proceedings would be taken to punish the perpetrators of the last massacre here I, in common with the bulk of the residents, trusted sufficient precautions would be taken to prevent any possibility of a failure in the administration of justice: but what do we find? After a lot of money has been spent in investigating the matter, the sub-inspector goes scot-free, while five poor ignorant blackfellows, who are presumed to have obeyed the white man's instructions, are committed for trial for wilful murder. What a farce is all this. The Government sent up here a detective officer to take charge of the case, and there was no scarcity of evidence for him to collect; but what was the use? Everything that could be done to burke the matter was done by those whose duty it was to assist Detective Barry. I am surprised that after the gross miscarriage of justice in the Californian Creek affair the Government did not have some knowledge of how things are managed here. I trust that this matter will not be allowed to rest without another inquiry being made. Apologising for trespassing so much on your space. Northern Resident. Herberton, January 22.[85]

In February 1885, a deputation, consisting of Messrs. D. Patience,

---

84 *Telegraph* 2 February 1885 p 2.
85 *Telegraph* 3 February 1885 p 2.

PUBLIC COMMENT

W.H. Hobson, and Walsh, of Cairns, interviewed the Premier and urgently requested that a native police camp should be permanently stationed in the Cairns district. Mr. Griffith replied that he would confer with the Chief Commissioner of Police upon the subject, who should have his early attention, and he would inform them of the result.[86] The Progress Association forwarded a largely signed petition to Brisbane for native police protection. Inspector Isley had closed the police reserve station, and the police horses were advertised to be sold by auction on 22 March 1885.[87] A largely attended meeting of the Cairns Progress Association was held on 28 July 1885, at New Tattersall's Hotel, Mr. D. Patience in the chair. The urgent necessity for police protection for the settlers against the blacks was discussed, and the unsatisfactory reply of the Commissioner of Police on the subject of the formation of a native police camp. Mr. Patience said, that when in Brisbane he had with others interviewed Mr. Griffith on the subject, and found the Premier altogether averse to the native police force, and anxious to abolish it, he therefore thought it would be useless to apply again for the establishment of such a force in this district. The urgent need of some protection being afforded the settlers was admitted by all present, so it was agreed to apply simply for police protection, leaving out the word "native," and accordingly Mr. Rodda moved—"That the secretary be instructed to address a letter to the Premier, bringing under his notice the necessity for establishing a police camp on the Mulgrave River for the protection of the settlers of the district against the depredations of the blacks. Seconded by Mr. Severin and carried.[88]

---

86 *Cairns Post* 26 February 1885 p 3.
87 *Telegraph* 21 March 1885 p 2.
88 *Cairns Post* 30 July 1885 p 2.

THE IRVINEBANK MASSACRE

PARLIAMENTARY PROCEEDINGS.

Mr. Edward Palmer (member for Burke) moved the adjournment of the House to call attention to an extract from the *Northern Standard*, which appeared in the *Courier* of the 14th instant, with reference to the shooting of two aboriginals on a charge of murdering two white men. He said the blacks who murdered the two white men, were deserving of death, but it had not been proved that the two aboriginals shot for the murder were the perpetrators of the crime. He also stated that Sub-Inspector Nichols, who had the two blacks shot, was rather fond of shooting, as he believed that he had on a previous occasion shot some blacks for no reason at all. He thought that some further notice should be taken of the matter. From the extract it appears that some troopers were out looking for the murderers of the two white men when they came across some blacks camping, one of whom was shot while asleep. Another jumped over a precipice and escaped, although fired at by the troopers. Two gins and a piccaninny who remained in the camp were then put to death and the remains burnt.

The Premier said, in reply, that a report had been made to him and he immediately ordered a strict inquiry to be made, but he had not yet received the report; when he did, he would lay it on the table.

Sir T. McIlwraith said he was glad to hear steps were being taken in the matter, and said he was horrified at the remarks of Mr. Palmer with reference to shooting the natives. During Sir Arthur Palmer's administration, a number of charges had been brought forward, but had been proved groundless.

The Minister for Lands denied that all the charges had proved groundless, and said that he knew of several that were proved to a moral certainty. After some further discussion the motion for adjournment was negatived.[89]

QUESTION

Mr. Norton asked the Colonial Secretary. Have the Government received confirmation of the reported murder of blacks near Irvinebank, in the Herberton district? If so, do the Government propose to institute any criminal proceedings in connection with that alleged gross outrage?

The Colonial Secretary (Hon. S. W. Griffith) replied. The Government have received the evidence taken at an inquiry held into the reported murder referred to, from which it appears that a murder was, in fact, committed. The evidence is however, incomplete and unsatisfactory and further inquiries are being made into the matter. 2. I trust the hon. gentlemen will excuse me from at present answering the second question.[90]

---

89 The Week 22 November 1884 p 9. Legislative Assembly, Hansard 18 November 1884, abridged.
90 Hansard 18 December 1884 p 1961.

6

Academic Treatment

The murder of four Aborigines on the night of 18 October 1884 at Irvinebank was not a signal event in the colonial history of Australia. The event, however, has become a matter of parochial interest to the community of Irvinebank. The fact that the murdered Aborigines were murdered by other Aborigines is, indeed, unremarkable in itself. However, some modern commentators have highlighted or perhaps, even overstated a dimension to the event that has brought the incident into the contemporary view of Australian colonial history.

Perhaps the first academic coverage of the Irvinebank Massacre was published by Noel Loos in his book, *Invasion and Resistance*, ANU Press, Canberra, 1982. Loos offered the following analysis of the incident:

> The Nigger Creek Native Police detachment was removed after its involvement in the murder of a group of pacified Aborigines became publicly known. When the Police Commissioner decided not to replace the detachment, a protest meeting was called. A numerously signed petition claimed that the earlier Aboriginal attacks on the mining field to the west of the rainforest had ceased following the

placing of the detachment at Nigger Creek. It was feared these would be renewed as miners and settlers were scattered for forty miles around Herberton. Moreover, the settlers believed the Native Police patrols from the Mulgrave and Johnstone Rivers and the new rush to the Johnstone would drive the Aborigines to the Herberton District and inhibit the development of recent mineral discoveries. Because of the close settlement of this area, the Police Commissioner thought trackers stationed at the ordinary police stations at Herberton, Watsonville, and Irvinebank would suffice. In April 1885, the Tinaroo Progress Association of Herberton informed the Colonial Secretary that 'depredations' had increased alarmingly since the departure of the Native Police detachment; miners and settlers would be forced to leave the district and one settler already had. Travellers on the road to Cairns were occasionally threatened and selectors' crops were being destroyed and their cattle speared, while huts were frequently robbed. At this stage the residents were still demanding more Native Police protection. The police inspector at Port Douglas informed the Police Commissioner objectively: It must be borne in mind that as the axe of the white man gradually but surely destroys the strongholds of the natives, so are outrages likely to increase as their scope gets narrower and narrower.' The pressure on the encircled rainforests was thus increasing. From 1885 till early 1889, the pages of the *Herberton Advertiser* and the *Cairns Post* are studded with reports of horses and bullocks killed, sheds, huts, and houses broken into and robbed, camps robbed, and crops of corn and potatoes stolen. Occasionally settlers were 'stuck up' and robbed.[91]

Then it seems keen local heritage enthusiasts in the 1990s took an interest in the local history of Irvinebank and obtained a government grant to carry out research and publish any findings or results that may have arisen from the efforts of the enthusiasts and their researchers. To that

---

91 *Invasion and Resistance, Aboriginal-European relations on the North Queensland frontier 1861-1897*, Noel Loos, ANU Press, Canberra, 1982, p 99, see also pp 60-61 & 105.

end, *Failure of Justice, The story of the Irvinebank Massacre* by Geof Genever was published by the Eacham Historical Society in 1999.[92] This work, in my opinion, would be better described as a parish pump publication covering the social history of Irvinebank and environs. The author, Terence Geoffrey Genever aka Geof Genever prior to authoring the above publication had completed at the James Cook University, Townsville the following theses:

> Black and blue: Aboriginal-police relations in Far North Queensland ... during the currency of The Aboriginals Protection and Restriction of the Sale of Opium Act 1897-1939 / by Terence Geoffrey Genever, 1992, and

> The road to Lotus Glen: Aborigines, the law, justice and imprisonment in colonial Queensland. PhD thesis, James Cook University of North Queensland, by Terence Geoffrey Genever, 1996.

Turning now to the *Failure of Justice*, the article is about 7000 words in length, structured as follows: a brief introduction, events in Irvinebank, the Inquest, Townsville hearing, summary and conclusion with end notes. Mr Genever, as a historian seems to document or portray the history of Australian Aborigines as being one of dispossession, exclusion and marginalisation by the process of colonisation with the added dimension that in response to colonisation, Australian Aborigines conducted a war of resistance. Hence, the following from his introduction:

> The North Queensland frontier, of which Irvinebank was part, was a dangerous place in the 1880s. Quite apart from anything else, a fitful war of resistance between the indigenous people and the white settlers had been going on for a long time. For the European it was

---

[92] *Failure of Justice: the story of the Irvinebank Massacre* / written by Geof Genever; additional information written by Duncan Ray, Tony Derksen [and] Henry Tranter, Malanda, Qld.: Eacham Historical Society, Reprint Second Edition, May 2010.

a case of colonisation and expansion; the Aboriginal people on the other hand, were fighting for survival and the removal of Europeans was often literally a matter of life or death to them. Therefore, it was understandable that they should fight against the invasion of their territory and this fact was acknowledged by some Europeans. Officially however, British settlement in Australia was not recognised as an invasion and the black people were declared to be fully subject to British law. This declaration made the defence of their homeland illegal. Their attacks on invading Europeans were classified as crimes rather than armed resistance by people who were trying to repel an invader.

We do not know how many died in this frontier conflict. Aboriginal deaths mostly went unrecorded and although fresh information is continually coming to light, we will never know the exact number of whites who died either. Many people simply disappeared without trace. Professor Noel Loos of James Cook University believes that over 300 Europeans may have died in North Queensland alone. Most historians accept that at least 10 Aborigines were killed for every white. However, Loos considers that 3000 Aboriginal dead would be a serious underestimation.[93]

The above may be interpreted as nothing more than leftist political orthodoxy having little basis in fact and no relevance to the subject matter of *Failure of Justice* but is trotted out as a political slogan and a necessary prelude to the narrative. Never at any stage in the article does Genever demonstrate, elucidate or connect the supposed murdering of the Aborigines at Irvinebank by Nigger Creek native troopers as an act in furtherance of war.

Therefore, it is no surprise that Genever ends the narrative with a typical piece of leftist political orthodoxy:

---

93 Ibid. p 7.

ACADEMIC TREATMENT

> The Native Mounted Police represented virtually the sum total of Colonial Queensland's policy towards its indigenous people for half a century and it was unarguably a policy primarily based on collective punishment without trial; one that was not only illegal, but morally bankrupt.[94]

He provides not a shred of evidence to support this statement. He persistently says the townspeople supported Nichols and constantly requisitioned the government of the day for relief from the depredations of the Aborigines. Yet he plucks this outlandish statement right out of his Little Red Book of left-wing aphorisms, without so much as a by your leave.[95] Of course, without rounding off the article with a hearty and robust slur on the white colonial past of Queensland, the job would not be complete.[96]

The crux of Genever's article is set out in the section called the Inquest. Genever has no legal qualifications so it is not surprising that his treatment of the legal proceedings and practises relating to the incident are inadequate. On the discovery of the bodies of the Aborigines, they were accorded the full rights of those of a white deceased found in similar circumstances. Initially an inquest was conducted on the bodies of the deceased Aborigines to determine the cause of death and whether there were any suspicious circumstances surrounding their death. The magistrate found that the supposed cause of death of the four Aborigines

---

94 Ibid. p 16.
95 The original Little Red Book or Quotations from Chairman Mao - contains 267 aphorisms from the Communist Chinese leader, covering subjects such as class struggle, "correcting mistaken ideas" and the "mass line", a key tenet of Mao Zedong Thought. Included is Mao's famous remark that "political power grows out of the barrel of a gun".
96 I urge the reader to refer back to the editorial of the *Telegraph* of 3 January 1885 at page 84 above.

was that they were killed by troopers of the Nigger Creek NP detachment.

Genever says, "The evidence from this inquest was forwarded to the Attorney-General in Brisbane who ordered that a criminal investigation take place at the Police Court in Herberton to see if Nichols and the troopers should stand trial in the Supreme Court." This statement demonstrates complete and utter ignorance of the Queensland criminal justice system. Under the administration of justice in the colony of Queensland, the police were charged with investigating crimes and were under the control of the Colonial Secretary. While Courts of criminal jurisdiction conducted trials of accused persons; they did not conduct criminal investigations. On the other hand, committal hearings were held to determine whether or not there was a reasonable possibility that a reasonable jury, properly instructed, would convict. This was called the 'prima facie test'. If not, the magistrate must immediately order the defendant's discharge.[97]

Genever then goes on to say the following:

> Clearly, the troopers could speak at least some English and it would have been surprising if they had been unable to. Why, one wonders, were they not interrogated by either Mowbray or Barry during the Committal Hearing? Magistrate Mowbray said that Dwyer's evidence regarding the capture of Spoopendyke when he bit the trooper's hand and his subsequent removal by native police was irrelevant. There is however a possibility that Spoopendyke and Toby were taken away somewhere and shot, in which case it would have been highly relevant. In any event it is strange that the Police Magistrate should have made no attempt to find out what happened to them. There are several features of Mowbray's conduct during both the inquest and

---

97 The reader is invited to refer back to page 47. One of the hoary criticisms of Joh Bjelke-Petersen by leftists was that he did not understand the doctrine of the Separation of Powers. Genever doesn't understand it either.

the committal hearing that raise questions.[98]

This paragraph clearly suggests that Genever had no legal training. Once a person has been arrested and charged, he is not obliged to answer any questions; furthermore, neither are the police nor the courts permitted to interrogate accused persons. This sort of ignorance on behalf of Genever must raise doubts about his ability to handle the material and, any inferences or conclusions, he might draw from the material. Further on he states, "It is also interesting that Sedgewick who heard the rifle fire on the night of the murders should tell the court that "he had a fair idea what the shooting was about", but was not asked to elaborate on his statement by Mowbray." Once again Genever reveals his ignorance of legal principals. A witness is only permitted to give evidence of what he directly knows. A witness is not permitted to give hearsay or speculative evidence. Further on still, Genever says, "It should also be remembered that if convicted, Nichols faced a substantial sentence as an accessory." This statement is blatantly incorrect. The law at that time stated that the punishment of an accessory before the fact was the same as the principal offender which meant Nichols, on conviction, would have been hanged by the neck until dead.

Genever's work is a longwinded, rambling, confused piece of prose. He ignores the fact that there were two committal proceedings and mixes the two at will, depending on what issue he might want to canvass. He is without legal training but charges in where angels fear to tread. He thrashes round the subject like a bull in a china shop and comes up smelling of roses.

---

98 Ibid. p 12.

The next author to deal with the Irvinebank incident is Jonathan Richards in his thesis *"A Question of Necessity": The Native Police of Queensland*, PhD thesis, Griffith University, 2005. Richards writes as follows:

> In 1885 a detachment commanded by Sub Inspector William Nichols and Cadet Roland Garraway killed six Aboriginal people at Irvinebank. Geof Genever's work on the killings is, to date, one of the few detailed studies of frontier violence in Queensland.[1] He says the Native Police virtually represented 'the sum total of Colonial Queensland's policy towards its indigenous people', and concluded, 'it was unarguably a policy primarily based on collective punishment without trial: one that was not only illegal, but morally bankrupe.[2] One European witness at the inquest said he saw black troopers riding about and 'the blacks scattered in all directions'. He then saw a blackfellow handcuffed and fastened to a fence, who 'was screaming out loud. Shortly after that the troopers led him away fastened between two horses'. According to one newspaper, 'over fifty persons had seen the bodies' at a camp near the town.[3] Several residents said the Native Police had burnt the bodies. Mine-owner John Moffat, a most reputable witness, testified: 'I found the remains of a large fire that had been made on the spot where the bodies formerly lay'.[4] Nichols was dismissed from the force and charged with murder, but the Crown did not proceed with the case. One police officer remarked before the preliminary hearing that local prejudice would obstruct further proceedings in the matter. 'If tried in Cooktown justice might be defeated owing to hatred of aboriginals'.[5]

> 1. Inquest into deaths of four Aborigines at Irvinebank, 23 October 1884, JUS/N110/84/511; Geof Genever, Failure of Justice (Eacham: Eacham Historical Society, 1996).

> 2. Genever, Failure of Justice, 16.

> 3. 'Alleged Slaughter of Aborigines', *Brisbane Courier* (14 November 1884: 5).

> 4. JUS/N110/84/511.

> 5. Detective John Barry to Officer In Command of Detectives, 17 January 1885, Police Staff File, William Austin Nichols, A/40104.[99]

Mr Richards does not contribute to the understanding of the incident but unscrupulously distorts the event even further than Genever's work. To demonstrate his lack of detail, Richards says that "In 1885 a detachment commanded by Sub Inspector William Nichols and Cadet Roland Garraway killed six Aboriginal people at Irvinebank." This sentence is riddled with errors. Six Aborigines were not killed; the bodies of four Aborigines were found at Irvinebank. Two Aborigines, Spoopendyke and Toby disappeared. There was no proof of their death. Moreover, the detachment of native police was not under the joint command of Nichols and Garraway. At the relevant time, Nichols was in sole command as the officer in charge. Furthermore, Garraway was never charged with any offence arising out of the incident, let alone murder. Richards then goes on to say, "Nichols was ... charged with murder, but the Crown did not proceed with the case." This statement is errant nonsense. Nichols was charged with being an accessory before the fact to the murder of the four Irvinebank Aborigines. Then Richards trots out the following, "If tried in Cooktown justice might be defeated owing to hatred of aboriginals." The full quote is as follows:

> Detective J Barry, Herberton to OIC Detectives, Brisbane, 17 January 1885: Re troopers and Nichols cases commence Monday, my opinion sure (of) committal; consider my duty to state that if tried in Cooktown, justice might be defeated owing to hatred of aboriginals there. Please instruct police magistrate here if think it necessary.[100]

---

99 "A Question of Necessity": *The Native Police of Queensland*, by Jonathan Richards, PhD thesis, Griffith University, 2005 pp 277-278.
100 QSA ID564169, Nichols staff file.

The statement is nothing more than pre-trial puff and bluster by an advocate trying to sound confident about the outcome of a trial. Moreover, it is only Barry's view that the people of Cooktown hated Aborigines. Nevertheless, after at least ten years of depredations by the Cape blacks, it may well have been difficult to find a Cooktown jury to convict a white man for shooting Aborigines.

As luck would have it, Mr Richards got another go at it. His second attempt is not much better and he once again muddies the water. He implies that Spoopendyke's body was among the four bodies that were burnt at Irvinebank. This is not the case. The fate of Spoopendyke was unknown. But to be fair to the man, I reproduce his second attempt per his book, *The Secret War*, University of Queensland Press, Brisbane, Reprint 2017:

> In October 1885, a detachment commanded by Sub-Inspector William Nichols and Cadet Roland Garraway killed at least six Aboriginal people at Irvinebank, inland from Cairns. A European witness saw 'the blacks scatter in all directions' after the troopers arrived. One 'blackfellow', handcuffed to a fence, 'was screaming out loud' before the troopers 'led him away fastened between two horses'. He and the others were never seen alive again, but their half-burned bodies were seen by many Europeans. According to the *Brisbane Courier* of 14 November 1884, 'over fifty persons had seen the bodies' at a camp near the town. Several residents said the Native Police had burnt the bodies. Mine-owner John Moffat, a most reputable witness, testified at the subsequent inquest: 'I found the remains of a large fire that had been made on the spot where the bodies formerly lay'.
>
> However, seeing evidence of racial violence and gaining a conviction were two different things. As one regional paper had written ten years before, 'You will never get a jury to bring in a verdict of murder for the killing of a black'. Nichols, dismissed from the force, was charged with 'being an accessory before the fact to

the Irvine Bank murders', but the Crown did not proceed with the case against him. One police officer remarked before the preliminary hearing that local prejudice would obstruct further proceedings in the matter, saying 'If tried in Cooktown justice might be defeated owing to hatred of aboriginals'! He was correct. W.M. Mowbray, the police magistrate at Herberton who conducted the inquest during October 1884 and the trial of Nichols in January 1885, was no friend to Aboriginal people. After Cadet Garraway gave his evidence at the court hearing, Mowbray declared 'there was not much use going on with the case', and discharged Nichols. The public applauded. Five troopers, tried in Townsville in April 1885 for 'having feloniously and wilfully killed and murdered at Irvine Bank', were discharged in October and transferred south. Historian Geof Genever's work on the killings, *Failure of Justice: The story of the Irvinebank Massacre* is one of the few detailed studies of a mass-killing incident in frontier Queensland. The Native Police, he says, virtually represented 'the sum total of Colonial Queensland's policy towards its indigenous people', and concluded, 'it was unarguably a policy primarily based on collective punishment without trial: one that was not only illegal, but morally bankrupt'.[101]

The next author to cover the incident was Timothy Bottoms who wrote as follows:

> ... Sub-Inspector William Austin Nichols who was based at Nigger Creek (now called Wondecla, south of Herberton), some 40 kilometres from the start of the fracas. Certainly, he was held responsible for his troopers killing 'two gins and a picaninny and a fellow called King Billy', around 8 p.m. on Saturday 18 October 1884. Sub-Inspector Nichols was 'suspended in consequence of circumstances in connection with the recent murders at Irvinebank'. White settlers had some sympathy for the Sub-Inspector, as Mrs Kate Atherton wrote to her daughter, Lucy: 'I suppose you will have

---

101 *The Secret War* by Jonathan Richards UQP, Brisbane, Reprint 2017 pp 33-34.

heard that poor Nichol[s] has been arrested ... we hear Garroway [sic] and the troopers were to be arrested also there is to be a hearing at Herberton[.] Today Isley and Carr went up ... I hope there will not be anything done to them.' Kate Atherton's wish came true: Nichols was acquitted. It was not until 22 October 1885 that the troopers were discharged in Townsville, because no acceptable interpreters could be found. One Herberton correspondent wrote: 'the fate of Nichols will be the salvation of any amount of murderous niggers [sic].'

> Sub-Inspector Ronald Garraway took over from his 'disgraced' associate, Nichols, who had been dismissed.[102]

The next work arises out of an Australian Research Council (ARC) funded project entitled 'The Archaeology of the Native Mounted Police', which commenced in early 2016 and was completed in 2020. The article is a blog by Lynley Wallis entitled *William Nichols, The NMP and the Murder of Aboriginal People at Irvinebank in 1884* at Archaeology on the Frontier (archaeologyonthefrontier).[103] Her opening remarks sets the scene more than adequately, "In this post I review the Irvinebank massacre, drawing heavily on the **excellent** (emphasis added) work of historian Geoff Genever in his hard-to-find publication "Failure of Justice: The Story of the Irvinebank Massacre"."

Ms Wallis says her article is based on the work of Genever yet she lists in her references primary sources. I say this because her work contains errors of fact.

> Garraway had been visiting Nigger Creek from Baan Bero and, on the request of Nichols, had remained to assist with a patrol. **Fact Check: Garraway left Barron River NP to get a deserter, Charlie and was**

---

102 *Conspiracy of Silence, Queensland's frontier killing times* by Timothy Bottoms, Allen & Unwin, Sydney 2013 p 148.
103 https://archaeologyonthefrontier.com/2019/08/25/irvinebank/

directed by Isley to assist Nichols.[104]

A person (or persons) unknown (and possibly Nigger Creek camp keeper John Stewart – see later) had returned to the scene and re-stoked the fire so that it would fully destroy the then partially burned bodies. As noted by Genever (1999:13), Detective Barry "clearly recognised Stewart's evidence as either lying or obstructive and more or less told him so". Genever (1999:16) went one step further, to raise the possibility that it might have been Stewart, acting under orders from Nichols, who had been sent back to the scene to re-stoke the fire and ensure the bodies were fully burned. The four-year working relationship between Stewart and Nichols, who had previously been stationed together at Oak Park, might have been a factor here. **Fact Check: sheer speculation, no evidence to support this.**

There is no clear indication that Alecky gave evidence to the October 1884 inquiry, which is not unusual given that Aboriginal people were rarely called as witnesses for various reasons, such as their testimony not being considered 'reliable', their inability to fully comprehend the legal context of the situation, or language difficulties in the English-speaking system. Further, the strong testimony of leading figure John Moffat would likely have been seen as adequate at the time; it was certainly not known then that the case would end up in court with Nichols and the trooper being formally charged over the killings. **Fact Check: Mowbray, "I attempted at this time (12/11/1884) to examine the aboriginal Alick, whose evidence should be the most important but was unable to obtain any intelligible statement from him."[105]**

It was about a month later, on 12 and 15 January 1885 that Nichols and the troopers involved were arrested by Townsville-based Detective, John Barry. **Fact Check: On 3 January 1885, Barry arrested William Nichols. Six troopers arrested on 11 January 1885 and Carlo**

---

104 QSA ID348709 folio 64.
105 QSA ID348709 folio 3.

arrested on 19 January 1885.[106]

By and large, the above represents the sum total of the attempts by academics to give a coherent and honest assessment of what has come to be known as the Irvinebank massacre. As professional historians, I must say the above is an abysmal attempt at accurately and precisely recounting the facts of the incident. None of the above could be described as a well written historical narrative. As to their ability at historical analysis and interpretation, it is non-existent. All of the above academics belong to the Black Armband school of thought which in turn limits their ability and skill at historical analysis and thus they are doomed to suffer from tunnel vision whilst compelled to recite meaningless leftist political slogans.

---

106 QSA ID847145.

7

Conclusion

The Irvinebank incident of 18 October 1884 was a simple event but a bloody one and if there had been no whites involved, it would have been nothing more than the re-enactment of an age-old happening of common occurrence among Aborigines since time immemorial. Great enmity existed between the disparate tribes of Australia. However, the allegation is that the murderers were in the service of the colony of Queensland and therefore, their white masters must bear if not all the liability, then at least some of it. To understand the incident, one has to look at the lead-up to the incident and post events. The principal actors were Sub-Inspector William Nichols and his native troopers who were located at the Nigger Creek native police camp.

THE IRVINEBANK MASSACRE

Timeline

15 October 1884: Nichols started on patrol at 9.20am with troopers Sambo, Sandy and Carlo from Nigger Creek NP camp. George William Seaman placed Nichols and troopers at Irvinebank taking Spoopendyke and Toby into custody.

16 October 1884: Nichols and trooper Sandy returned to Nigger Creek camp at 11.30am, while Sambo and Carlo returned at 9.20am with deserter Charlie from Barron River NP camp. Cadet Garraway from Barron River NP camp also arrived at Nigger Creek NP camp.

17 October 1884: Nichols and trooper Sandy started on patrol while troopers Sambo, Pituri, Carlo, Larry and Charlie started at 7.30am. Cadet Garraway obtained Inspector Isley permission to accompany Nichols on patrol. Seaman placed Nichols and troopers at Irvinebank and that night they camped at Irvinebank. Garraway confirmed this.

18 October 1884: Garraway confirmed troopers paraded and instructed by Nichols to "Catch Tommy and mind you don't use your rifles." Corroborated by GW Seaman, "After being marshalled, they left the camp on horseback." Troopers were sent out on their own without the command of a white office. Nichols and Garraway remained at the Irvinebank camp.

19 October 1884: Nichols, Garraway and troopers return to Nigger Creek camp. Partially burnt bodies of four Aborigines found at a site near Irvinebank. John Moffat deposed that Alicky had taken him to a mountain top Sunday morning between 9 and 10 am and the bodies appeared to have been dead 12 to 15 hours.

22 October 1884: Const Moroney visited the scene of the murder on top of a mountain, near Irvinebank and saw the remains of four Aborigines partially burnt and decomposed.

23 October 1884: W Mowbray PM and Const Moroney attended the murder scene and found a heap of ashes and some wood, bodies destroyed.

CONCLUSION

From the above timeline there are three distinct incidents:

1. The arrest of Spoopendyke and Toby and their disappearance on 15 October 1884.

2. The murder of four Aborigines on top of a mountain in the vicinity of Irvinebank on the night of 18 October 1884.

3. The destruction of the bodies of the murdered Aborigines on the night of 22 October 1884.

Turning to the first incident of 15 October 1884, this event is discrete and stands on its own and is in no way linked to the subsequent two incidents. Spoopendyke and Toby were arrested by Nichols who had warrants for their arrest. On the information available, Nichols said he discharged them without taking them before a magistrate, but the prisoners were never seen again.[107] The only offence that appears to have been committed by Nichols was failing to take the prisoners before a Magistrate as soon as convenient. Nichols would also be in breach of police regulations such as failing to uphold the law and failing to record his presence at Irvinebank in his Native Police Monthly Report for October 1884.[108]

The second incident of 18 October 1884 was the finding of the bodies of four Aborigines whose cause of death was unknown, thus requiring an inquest on the bodies. An inquest was duly held and suspicion fell on the Native Police detachment then at Irvinebank. On the recommendation of

---

107 QSA ID564169, folio 14, Nichols' Staff File.
108 QSA ID847145. Isley, Troopers' Committal: The officers send in monthly returns of duty. Sub-Insp Nichols did not send any return of his having been Irvinebank. He sent in a monthly report for October. See also Hansard LA, 18 November 1884, p 1441.

the Attorney-General, the police were asked to investigate the matter. As a consequence, seven native troopers were arrested and charged with the murder of the four Aborigines. They were then taken before a police magistrate for committal proceedings who found that a prima facie case was made out against the prisoners by witnesses entitled to a reasonable degree of credit. The magistrate committed the prisoners to stand their trial at the next sitting of the Supreme Court at Townsville and they were remanded into custody. The police also arrested and charged Nichols with being an accessory before the fact. The magistrate found at Nichols' committal hearing that there was insufficient evidence to commit Nichols and he was discharged. However, evidence was given by Isley that Nichols had committed an error of judgment.

The third incident of 22 October 1884, destroying or disposing of the bodies, this does not appear to have been considered, at the time of the murders, as attracting any sort of criminal liability. Barry at no stage questioned anyone about it. The disposing of the bodies by burning does not seem to appear in any of the correspondence or reports as constituting a criminal act.[109] Constable Denis Moroney visited the murder site on 22 October 1884 but does not seem to have been instructed to secure and guard the site; when he returned the next day with the police magistrate, the bodies had been destroyed and reduced to ashes. Mowbray at the inquest saw it as a circumstance confirming the deaths of the four Aborigines as unlawful. Some legally unqualified commentators have bandied about the idea that certain parties should have been charged with being an accessory after the

---

109 See Edward Palmer, the member for Burke, Legislative Assembly, Hansard 18 November 1884 p 1442: There is no doubt, from the burning of the bodies, that the persons concerned had some idea that what they had done was not consonant with their duties at all as a police force.

fact, to wit disposing of the bodies. The two prime suspects are Nichols and Constable John Stewart. No evidence has been offered for this allegation. The only credible evidence I can find is the following entries in the Nigger Creek NP Day Journal:

> 22 October 1884 Sub-Insp Nichols office duty, Const Stewart started on patrol at 7am also troopers Sambo, Carlo & Pituri; Const McInerney camp duty, Tpr Larry horse duty, horses mustered, gins general useful, issued blankets.
>
> 23 October 1884 Sub-Insp Nichols office duty, Const Stewart & trooper returned to camp; Const McInerney camp duty, Tpr Larry stable duty, horses mustered, gins general useful.[110]

These entries merely suggest that Stewart and the three troopers had an opportunity to sneak back and totally destroy the bodies but the matter was never followed-up.

The next question is why was Nichols neglectful or negligent in his command of the Nigger Creek NP camp? Seymour's opinion of Mr Nichols was as follows, "had the character of being a willing hard-working officer during his nine years' service and no complaints of misconduct or harsh treatment of blacks has ever been made against him." On his posting to Nigger Creek in 1882, Nichols applied for three months leave and said "during the last three months I have had particularly heavy duty to perform having been continually in the saddle without hardly a day's respite." The modern approach to staff reviews in police or military establishments, where staff have failed or under preformed, is to adopt a psychosocial study of their background and needs. To that end, their service history is usually looked

---

110 QSA ID86147 Police Camps Cook.

at to see if the subject was exposed to or suffered any traumatic events.

On 14 September 1881, Sub-Inspector Henry Pollock Kaye was speared though the heart by the blacks at Woolgar and died instantly. Nichols said, "I left Mr Kaye when I last saw him alive within two miles and a half of our camp. His body was lying about half-a mile nearer my camp. I saw a wound on the right breast; it had not penetrated the other side, a very small wound. It was a spear wound; the body was warm but quite dead. Mr Kaye had no arms with him when I left him; his trooper had no arms. He was endeavouring to put confidence into the blacks." Under modern conditions of service, Nichols would have been entitled to all sorts of medical, psychological and social assistance and counselling. The following is a contemporaneous description of Kaye's death:

> A short time elapsed before Mr. Nichols arrived on the scene, and I leave anyone to imagine what his feelings must have been. I believe Mr. Kaye's troopers were dreadfully distressed, and what they did— or what people say they did is a matter I am not able to write about. I may say this, however, that as much as Mr. Nichols could do in conformity with his duty he did; and I think the occurrence has cast a terror over the district. ... A few words about sub-inspector Nichols and those who assisted in rendering the last tribute to the departed gentleman. Mr. Nichols was most persevering and energetic in bringing to light the perpetrators of the crime, and has done all that can be done in this remote region to have the matter fully investigated. He rode to Georgetown after leaving the Woolgar in safety, and no doubt has sent in his official report to headquarters.[111]

Nichols' application for three months leave was fobbed off by Seymour, with a promise in the near future of a posting to Brisbane. Then in August

---

111   Brisbane Courier 19 October 1881 p 3.

CONCLUSION

1884, Isley and Nichols had a particularly acrimonious exchange of letters with the Commissioner over Nichols' failure to complete and lodge particular camp returns and vouchers relating to June 1884. Isley said Nichols was neglectful and careless and wanted Nichols disciplined. To which the Commissioner replied stop his pay until the matter resolved. Nichols informed the Commissioner he objected to the slur by Isley and that his returns were in order and any delays were caused by his having to patrol the Russell River and the fact that he had been sick with fever. He also asked for a transfer from the district. Isley and Sgt Breene made a spot check on the Nigger Creek NP camp on 28 September 1884 and wrote in the Day Journal of the Nigger Creek NP camp the following, "28 September 1884, visited this camp; inspected no books owing to absence of Sub-Insp Nichols. I cannot however speak too highly of the cleanliness and proper order of the camp."

The incident of 18 October 1884 involving the death of four Aborigines at Irvinebank was described by Isley as "an error of judgment to send out so large a party of troopers without an officer in charge of them and not a neglect of duty." The premise behind the native police was that they were useful against wild blacks but white officers were needed to control and restrain their atavistic blood lust; without a Christian education, the blacks lacked the moral, legal and ethical constraints of civilisation. The premise is adequately illustrated by the following exchange:

> 28. Do you think it would be of any use to send a number of white men to capture blacks? Yes, under officers that are good bushmen. If the object of the Native Police is merely the destruction of the aborigines, they are a most efficient force for that purpose. If you want to destroy the blacks by wholesale slaughter, you could not find people

more suited for the purpose than the Native Police.[112]

The premise was never spoken of; and it is best illustrated by the following quote from the 1861 Select Committee Native Police Force Report:

> It is clearly shown by the evidence of the Commandant and some of the witnesses, that any want of discipline that has existed in this Force, or any excesses that are attributable to the Troopers, have arisen mainly from the inefficiency, the indiscretion, and the intemperate habits of some of the Officers, rather than from any defect in the system itself.[113]

A sharper edge was put on the policy behind the Native Police by a correspondent to the *Palmer Chronicle* of 20 December 1884:

> In the case of the poor wretches shot down at Herberton no doubt a serious offence has been committed; inasmuch as those who suffered were known to be inoffensive; and their massacre can be nothing than deliberate and cold-blooded murder. There was not even the circumstances of excitement and pursuit to justify the instance of official savagery. But surely those in power in the Colonial Office and in the Police Department, are not simple enough to expect it believed that supposing these unfortunate wretches to have been the Walsh murderers, or their accessories that when found they would have been brought in alive; and indulged with the farce of a formal trial. Whatever those in high places may affect, it is well known that the directory of police never intend or encourage any such whimsical nonsense. They may flaunt their official morality in the Assembly, and before Southern constituencies when cases of such flagrant outrages are exposed to public view; and whatever their official instructions may be in such cases, it is a well-known fact that there is a private and unwritten code of instructions understood and practised by the Native Police that aboriginal criminals are not to be taken prisoners,

---

112 Legislative Assembly Qld Select Committee Native Police Force Report, 1861 p 83.
113 Ibid., p 2. Flying is dangerous but aircraft are useful. Air disasters are rare and caused by pilot error not mechanical failure.

CONCLUSION

but to be shot down whenever and wherever found. Shooting criminal niggers only becomes a crime when officers do not do it thoroughly and secretly. No one here ever supposed for a moment that the Walsh Murderers would ever be brought to trial and in fact they knew when the police returned from their search that Jedburgh law[114] had been enforced.[115]

From a nineteenth century perspective, Nichols was no longer a good chap, a white man; he had gone troppo and let the team down. Consequently, he was dismissed from the force with the princely sum of £7. 8s. 6d. From a modern perspective, Nichols appears to have made a cry for help. The system fobbed him off and then Nichols fell into a steady neglect of his duties, perhaps even dereliction of duty, thus the Irvinebank incident.

Turning now to the native troopers, assuming they killed the four Irvinebank Aborigines, does any blame, moral, legal or otherwise, attach to them? Under the English legal system no one is immune from the law. Consequently, they were arrested and committed to stand their trial in the Supreme Court at Townsville but they were discharged for want of prosecution. No motive for their actions appears anywhere in the source material but there is the following opinion from Archibald Meston:

> I am quite satisfied that Sub-inspector Nichols had nothing to do with it. He is one of the most efficient and faithful officers in the whole police force. Every officer of native police knows that his troopers, under certain circumstances, will go off on little excursions of their own and slaughter all ages and sexes indiscriminately. The officer may only hear accidentally long afterwards what was done

---

114 According to which a man was hanged first and tried afterward.
115 See appendix A below.

during the expedition.[116]

The troopers were under the control of Corporal Sambo; the following is a brief background on Sambo:

> Trooper 'Sambo' or 'Sam Pootingah' was a well-known Native Police scout and interpreter on the frontier with over ten years' experience in dealing with hostile Aborigines." Nicholls teamed up with Kaye on the Woolgar purely by chance.
>
> 'Sam Pootingah' alias 'Ferriter', also known by the derogatory term 'Sambo', led an interesting life. He was a childhood friend to Tom Petrie, and had joined the Native Police in 1852 on reaching manhood. He deserted many times and was implicated in many thefts, and was suspected of the murder of a known Aboriginal murderer named 'Piper' in the Gympie area. Like many other Native Police troopers, he was recruited from the gaols to serve out his sentence in the far north of Queensland. He accompanied Wentworth D'Arcy Uhr to Burketown in 1865, and served with Arthur Johnstone in the Herbert River detachment in the early 1870s until Johnstone banished him from the Townsville region when Sam deserted in 1874. Good troopers were hard to find and 'Sam' was back in the service by 1878.[117]

Trooper Sambo was at the side of Sub-Inspector Kaye on the Woolgar when he was speared and killed by the blacks. Is it, therefore, possible to draw Sambo into the web of Nichols' malingering or mental breakdown? Is it perhaps, too long a bow to draw, to suggest that Sambo through bonding and loyalty to Nichols, together with Nichols acquiescence, somehow became aware of Nichols malaise or disaffection and sensed that Nichols had come adrift or disconnected from the system? And thinking he was helping

---

116 Brisbane Courier 27 December 1884 p 3; see p 45 above. Archibald Meston (26 March 1851 – 11 March 1924) was an Australian politician, civil servant, journalist, naturalist and explorer.
117 Hillier Alan J, The Native Police under Scrutiny, Journal of the Royal Historical Society of Queensland volume 15 issue 6: pp. 279-293.

CONCLUSION

Nichols, became a psychological crutch. In effect became the head of an unofficial hierarchy at the Nigger Creek camp and effectively took over Nichols' role? Or was it just Black on Black violence, bred out of tribal enmity?

Nichols' failure of command is obvious. If he had been present, then Tommy may have been apprehended and lines of inquiry followed up. However, Nichols abdicated his command and handed it over to Corporal Sambo. Was it wilful negligence, professional misconduct or was it some psychological disorder?

What was the reaction of the Government to the Irvinebank incident? On a bureaucratic level, the administrative arm of government purged the police of the offending parties. Sub-Inspector William Nichols was dismissed with no entitlements and the troopers were also dismissed. The Nigger Creek native police camp was also closed and the Port Douglas police division was re-arranged as follows:

Cook Sub-Division D Port Douglas 1885[118]

Police Stations	Officers	NCOs & Constables	Native Troopers
Port Douglas	1	15	4
Barron River	1	2	5
Cairns		4	1
Herberton		8	1
Irvinebank		2	
Mossman River	1	1	5
Mulgrave River		2	
Thornborough		2	1
Watsonville		2	

The executive arm of government also employed the criminal justice

---
118 Report of Commissioner of Police 1885, dated 6 July 1886, Table A.

system to have the offending parties tried and convicted for the criminal activities alleged to have occurred during the Irvinebank incident but they failed.

On a government or policy level, the Premier, Sir Samuel Griffith, in the Supply debate of 1885 said, hon. members would observe that the 128 native troopers provided for last year were now called "native trackers," indicating an intention on the part of the Government to make a change in the administration of the native police branch of the force. The system which had been adopted hitherto, by which a comparatively large number of native police were accompanied by only one white officer, was not at all satisfactory. He should be very glad if the Government could see their way to abolish the native police altogether, and there were many parts of the colony where they were no longer required where the work could be done quite as well and, in some respects, better by white men, except perhaps, tracking. There were, however, other parts of the colony, he was bound to admit having struggled all he could to see his way to abolish the native police altogether, where white troopers could not penetrate. For instance, in the northern jungles it was absolutely impossible for a white man to get through. It was, therefore, impossible to abolish them altogether, and what was proposed to be done was that in all cases at least two white police should be attached to every detachment of native police; and by degrees the whole system would be abolished. That was as far as he was at present able to see his way to make a change in the system. Very numerous complaints had been made of late from various parts of the North about the depredations by blacks, and urgent requests had been made that something should be done to prevent them; sometime it meant to be revenged upon them.

CONCLUSION

Where, however, lives had been taken something, of course, must be done; but the Premier did not think the native police ought to be employed to avenge the killing of cattle and horses. The Government had been unable to meet all the requests that had been made. It must not be forgotten that the progress of settlement in the North had been of such a nature as to destroy the food supply of the blacks to a very great extent, especially where they were very numerous; and it was not to be wondered at that they occasionally helped themselves to the settlers' stock. He could quite sympathise with them when they were suffering from starvation. Some of the stations there were left in charge of a stockman and a couple of blackboys, and the owners expected the native police to act as stock-riders for them. That was no part of the duties of the native police; and considering the owners were put to so little expense in managing their stations they might very fairly allow a bullock now and then to sustain the life of the aboriginal inhabitants, whose means of subsistence had been taken from them.

The Government was also endeavouring to make some arrangement for civilising the blacks in the northern parts of the colony. Overtures had been made by two missionary societies to render their services, but their proposals were not yet definite enough; he trusted, however, that before long a great deal would be done in that direction. At Cooktown and the neighbourhood, a start had been made, and a good many aborigines were now at work on the plantations. The difficulty was to get anything of that sort properly supervised. Under the heading of "Contingencies" there was an increase of £4,800, attributable to the increase in the number of police. The work could not be done for less money, and, comparing it with the expenditure last year, he believed it would cover the expense.

Mr. Palmer said that scarcely a single word of the Premier's had reached him, because he only addressed himself to those nearest to him. He would like the hon. gentleman to explain again the system on which the Native Police Force was to be continued. There was evidently to be a change, and he wanted to know what the change was.

The Premier (Sir Samuel Griffith) replied he endeavoured to explain that, as far as the arrangements had yet been made, it was proposed that at every station for native police there should be white policemen, and that the black trackers should be attached to the white police. The present system had been very different from that. The practice had been for a number of native troopers to go out into the bush accompanied by not more than one white man, and sometimes without even one, although he believed the instructions were that they should not be allowed to go out except in charge of white man. It was intended to assimilate the system as nearly as possible to that of the white police.

The Hon. J. M. Macrossan said he would like to know whether the camps for native troopers would be the same as hitherto, and whether it was intended that there should be two white constables with each detachment of native police in addition to the officer in charge?

The Premier replied there would always be two white constables at a camp, and sometimes a senior-constable would be in charge. There were to be the same camps or police stations, not in charge of an officer, but of a senior-constable or sergeant, with a smaller number of black trackers. The practice of the black police making raids through the country in times past would not be allowed any longer.

CONCLUSION

Mr. Palmer said he was afraid that, even with the proposed alteration in the system of the native police, if the native police were anxious to make raids through the country they would do so; they would lose or slip the white police as they had often lost their officers on previous occasions, of which the Herberton case was an instance. He was quite certain that the native police, if properly officered and properly looked after, could be made of great service in outside places, especially such districts as the York Peninsula district, which was now being settled and through which a telegraph line was being constructed. He believed that two or three detachments of police would be necessary to keep that line clear.

The Premier: That is an exceptional case.

Mr. Palmer: The great drawback hitherto had been not having officers who were enthusiastic in their work. Generally speaking, young and inexperienced officers were placed in charge of five or six troopers, and when they were out on patrol the officer lost control of the troopers. He thought some old experienced sergeants of the force would make better officers for the native police than the men who were usually appointed.[119]

Even a great legal mind such as Sir Samuel Griffith could find no way to rid the colony of Queensland of the native police.

---

119 LA Hansard 24 September 1885 p 825-826.

Appendix A

TO SHOOT OR NOT TO SHOOT THAT IS THE QUESTION.

The following extracts from a letter are copied from the *Palmer Chronicle* of the 20th December 1884.

I am a man of my opinions; and who have the courage to state them and stand by them when occasion calls. All the same, I see no reason in trumpery matters to flaunt those opinions in the face of opponents, for the sake of irritation or annoyance. In all things I like to take a medium stand; never either too much for or too much against.

I read with supercilious infidelity the charges heaped against the police in the House of Assembly; and I don't believe that the police are more cruel and inhumane than any other class of men; and I don't believe that they would shoot down inoffensive blacks. That they sometimes make a terrific havoc among the blacks when depredations are too rife to be overlooked, is certain and the heads of the Department know it; and the Colonial Secretary should also know it, if he don't. What on earth do they supply the native police with revolvers and so many pounds of ammunition for, if it is not to shoot? I have known blacks hunted and shot down with as much zest and cool enjoyment as if the blacks scurrying for bare life were so many wolves or other brute vermin; where regular black hunts were the order. But the sportsmen were not policemen; but outraged squatters, selectors and others. It is only a few weeks ago that I was asked to go and spend Christmas holidays on the Upper Mitchell, on a lonely wild name trackless run. I was assured by my friend that there would be plenty of good sport during the wet season. That there would be plenty of blacks to pot. Yet that man was not cruel or inhumane; but his heart had been rendered callous by the constant necessity of shooting down the blacks in self-preservation. He would not seek out, a black to shoot him. But when he found his cattle speared and scattered; and the tailing process rendered doubly arduous, or perhaps altogether void; when he found himself surrounded in his homestead by vast mobs of hungry, yelling, murderous demons; and his movement dogged and hemmed in on every side, and his life menaced every time he set his foot out of doors, then he found necessary to shoot; and the ruthless click of the snider sounds the sweet music of a relieving army to the besieged city. Every click, a shot, and every shot, a life. Yet under such circumstances who would not shoot? So much for one view of the subject!

We come now to view the subject from the stand point of those who look upon the snider as the most perfect civilising influence amongst the blacks. Whither the pharisaic anthropologist, who reads his Bible with the thoughts and feelings of superiority of the white man and thanks his stars that he is not as other races are, nor even as those poor aboriginals; or the Sadduceeic professors of the Darwinian theory who thank their zoophyte progenitors that their Species have had their origin and development from superior beginnings, are justified in their contempt for and usage of the aboriginals of Queensland, I will not here venture to determine. But it is certain that whatever their opinions or professions are they both act under given circumstances, with the same disregard of human life as exemplified in the blacks, as those who are not possessed by any of those esoteric sentiments. Self-preservation is the strongest instinct in all classes of men; and where that instinct alone sways, both great classes act upon the same principal and with like results, the extirpation of their inferior brethren, the aboriginals of the soil.

What a fine frenzy of human feeling ran through the Colonial Secretary's speech when he declared that he would have justice avenged on the poor niggers at Herberton. And yet that is the feeling which finds an echo in all southern colonists and stayers at home in England. But what good has the exuberance of Exeter Hall sentiments towards the poor black ever done for him. The rampant feeling of those prating knaves who sympathise so deeply with the injured aboriginal is mere sentiment and commotion; and their actual Ignorance of the demonic propensities and murderous cannibalism of the noble savage is unknown to them. In the economy of progressive life, Human and brute being is subject to the same irrevocable law—survival of the fittest. Inferior races and inferior life in all forms go to the walls; and their places in the economy of nature know them no more forever. And so, it is with the aboriginals of Queensland. They are a doomed race; and must sooner or later give place to the higher forms of human life, whatever the Aboriginal Preservation Societies and other institutions of kindred mawkish sentimentalists may say or do to the country.

Sympathy with and pity for the blacks is a comfortable and an easy sentiment to indulge when we have no interests which are affected by their depredations and property liable to be destroyed by their brutal instincts and their fiendish delight in destruction. But place those same sentimental agitators in the same relation to the blacks as occupied by squatters and others, where their life, their families and property, and stock are continually menaced, and daily liable to destructive raids; and their whimpering sentimentality and ignorant sympathy with the lowest form of human life will evaporate in self-preservation! and their high fraught sentiment would daily ooze out of their being with the same facile flow with which bodies in this climate exude with febrile softness.

I would not countenance the cold-blooded massacre of those human wretches; but their subjugation to law and order must be insisted upon. If the arm of the law as extended from Brisbane is too short, or its influence exerted at such a distance is too weak to keep their cannibal natures down and to confine them within their own savage haunts, and to control their inhuman behaviour, then the more active means, and more repressive measures of first settlers amongst aboriginals must be adopted by the squatters and graziers themselves.

In the case of the poor wretches shot down at Herberton no doubt a serious offence has been committed; inasmuch as those who suffered were known to be inoffensive; and their massacre can be nothing than deliberate and cold-blooded murder. There was not even the circumstances of excitement and pursuit to justify the instance of official savagery. But surely those in power in the Colonial Office and in the Police Department, are not simple enough to expect it believed, that supposing these unfortunate wretches to have been the Walsh murderers, or their accessories that when found they would have been brought in alive; and indulged with the farce of a formal trial.

Whatever those in high places may affect, it is well known that the directory of police never intend or encourage any such whimsical nonsense. They may flaunt their official morality in the Assembly, and before Southern constituencies when cases of such flagrant outrages are exposed to public view; and whatever their official instructions may be in such cases, it is a well-known fact that there is a private and unwritten code of instructions understood and practised by the Native Police that aboriginal criminals are not to be taken prisoners, but to be shot down whenever and wherever found. Shooting criminal niggers only becomes a crime when officers do not do it thoroughly and secretly. No one here ever supposed for a moment that the Walsh Murderers would ever be brought to trial and in fact they knew when the police returned from their search that Jedburgh law had been enforced.

If Mr Griffith is not aware of those facts, it is high time he should be enlightened. What more than a legal fiasco, calculated to bring law into contempt can result from putting black criminals on their trial. No case tried has ever obtained the conviction of the guilty black and it is perfectly well known up North that when any crime is committed whether of murder or outrage, calling for the interference of the police, that no prisoners will be brought in, and no trial ensue. The Police Magistrate may do the humbug of issuing warrants for the apprehension of the criminals; but it is with a perfect knowledge that they will never be put in force. If the police come across the suspect criminals they are shot down without further ado; and the legal fiasco of a set trial is dispensed with. Fancy a black prisoner whom the police are morally certain is the guilty one, and to whom all circumstances point, placed in the dock—the indictment is read, couched in all the obscure bombast of legal phraseology—The prosecutor launching out in all the frowsy eloquence of a fierce tirade, the twelve good men and true listening and looking like twelve pins, the learned judge shaking his bewigged head sitting with the patient attention of a stoic. The crucial point is reached of bringing the crime home to the prisoner, but he "bel" his interpreter, "bel" and the giggle of baffled justice titters through the court.

Even if a conviction were obtained under such negative circumstances it would be impossible to satisfy Public Opinion that the justice dealt was any more satisfactory than the Jedburgh law administered in the bush, with a policemen as public prosecutor, the black troopers as jurymen, and the snider as judge and executioner.

If Mr Griffith will enquire into these matters, he will find that he has allowed his feelings for outraged humanity in the case of blacks to run away with him and we fain hope that he will not seek to establish the legal fiascos of set trials in the case of criminal and offending blacks. The law is supposed to be purgative, but the only cure for black criminal is Fire!

In following up this subject to such a length I am not to be considered as defending the indiscriminate murder of the harmless and defenceless creatures. But I insist that cannibalism and lawless murders must be put down with a strong hand. Chinamen are the regular and helpless victims of cannibalism and every now and again Europeans fall victims to their fatal spear, and murderous tomahawk. Q. V.[120]

---

120 Herberton Advertiser 14 January 1885 Vol. V No. 4.

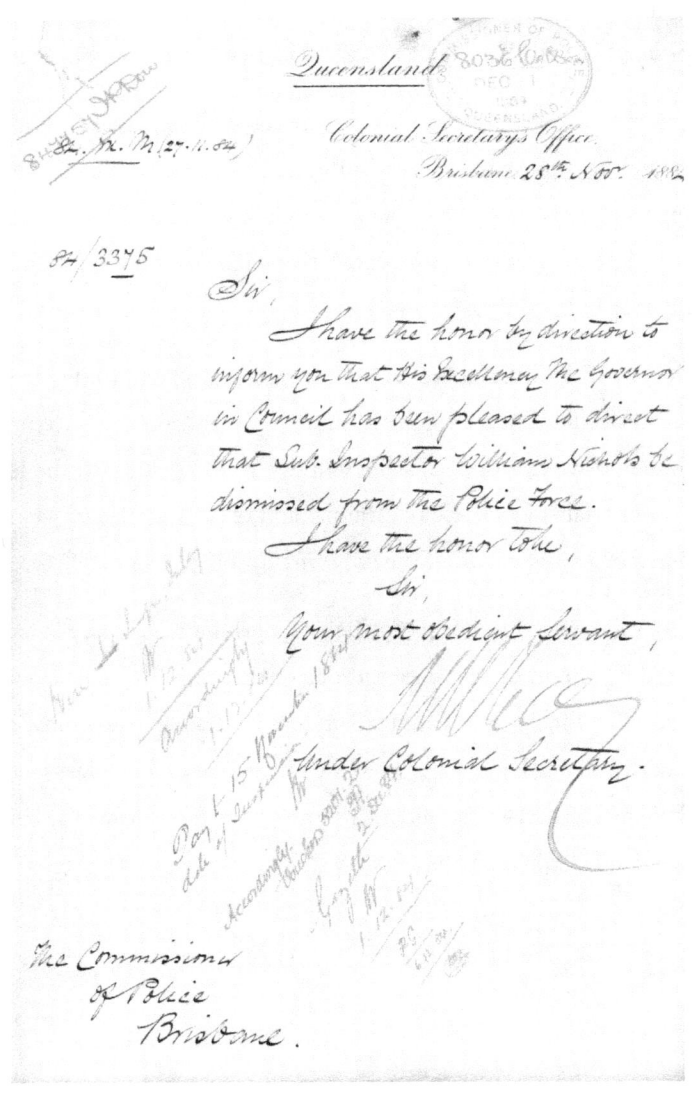

Dismissal of Sub-Inspector William Nichols

QSA ID564169, Nichols' Staff File

APPENDIX

Loudoun House, Irvinebank residence, 1886

It is the dwelling and office of John and Margaret Moffat's home, built in 1884.

(Courtesy of State Library of Queensland)

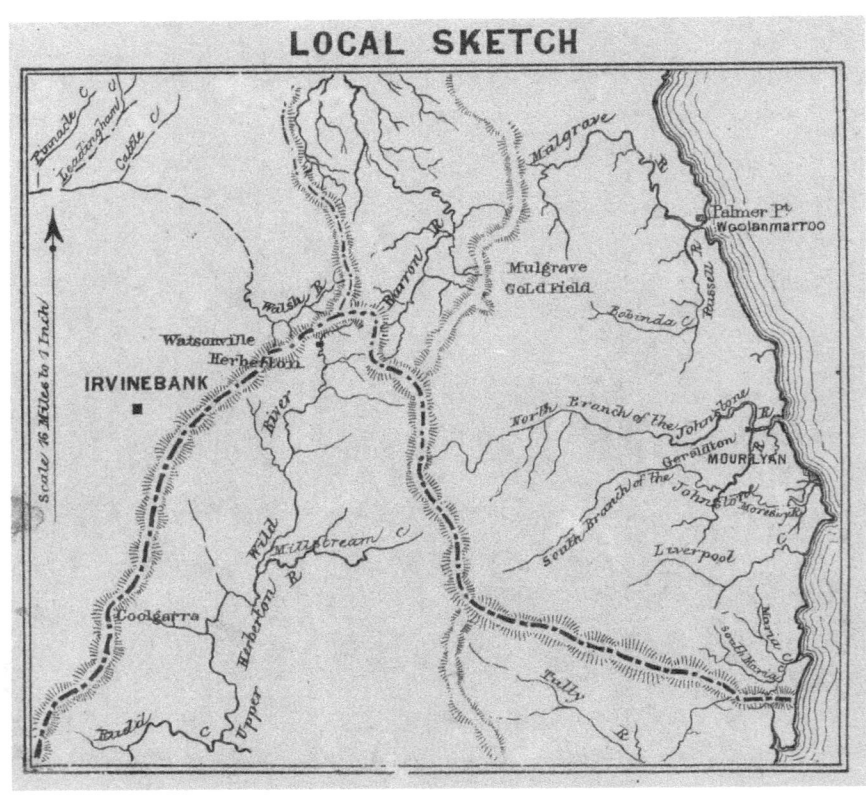

Courtesy of State Library of Queensland.

APPENDIX

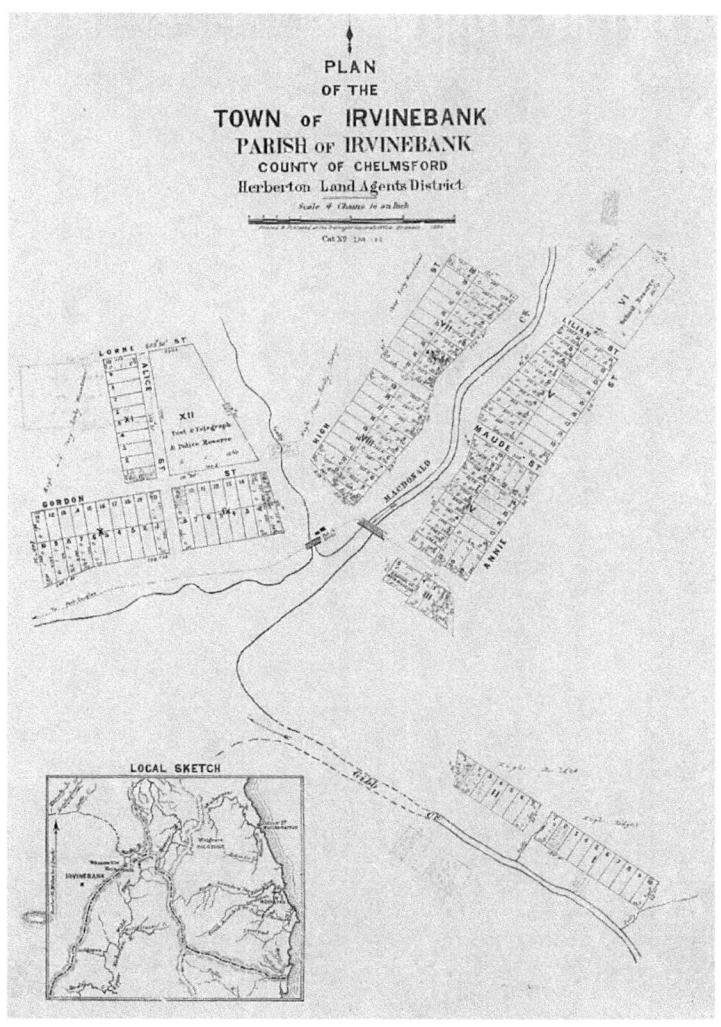

Courtesy of State Library of Queensland.

Bibliography

Bottoms, Timothy Conspiracy of Silence, Queensland's frontier killing times, Allen & Unwin, Sydney 2013.

Genever, Geof Failure of Justice: the story of the Irvinebank Massacre / written by Geof Genever; additional information written by Duncan Ray, Tony Derksen [and] Henry Tranter, Malanda, Qld.: Eacham Historical Society, Reprint Second Edition, May 2010.

Hillier Alan J The Native Police under Scrutiny, Journal of the Royal Historical Society of Queensland volume 15 issue 6.

Loos, Noel Invasion and Resistance, Aboriginal-European relations on the North Queensland frontier 1861-1897, ANU Press, Canberra, 1982.

Richards, Jonathan "A Question of Necessity": The Native Police of Queensland, PhD thesis, Griffith University, 2005.

Richards, Jonathan The Secret War, UQP, Brisbane, Reprint 2017.

Wallis, Lynley Blog entitled William Nichols, The NMP and the Murder of Aboriginal People at Irvinebank in 1884 at Archaeology on the Frontier (archaeologyonthefrontier).

Abbreviations

DTS	David Thompson Seymour
GG	Government Gazette
LA	Legislative Assembly
NP	Native Police
NMP	Native Mounted Police
PG	Police Gazette
PM	Police Magistrate
Qld	Queensland
QPG	Queensland Police Gazette
QSA	Queensland State archives
QSL	Queensland State Library

THE IRVINEBANK MASSACRE

THE IRVINEBANK MASSACRE

THE IRVINEBANK MASSACRE